Love the Ones Who Drive You Crazy

"One of my favorite pastimes is reading the sermons of preachers who have long since gone to their reward. And one of my least favorite realizations along the way has been that few of the churches these preachers once led so well survived much longer. In fact, some of the churches I have attended in my own lifetime—some of the churches where I was once taught so well—have already decayed and been disbanded. In so many cases, it was not false doctrine or false teachers that undermined the church but a simple failure to love—to maintain the unity of the Spirit in the bond of peace. It's for this reason I'm so grateful for this book and for Jamie Dunlop's clarion call for you—yes, you!—to pursue unity in your local church. May God use it to convict his people and protect his church."

Tim Challies, author, *Seasons of Sorrow*

"Needed! Yes, that's what I thought through reading each chapter of Jamie Dunlop's *Love the Ones Who Drive You Crazy.* I needed this book during four decades of pastoring. I need it now as a church member. Dunlop takes difficult situations we face in the local church and helps us see the power of Christ alone to truly love one another in Christ's body. I highly recommend this book!"

Phil A. Newton, Director of Pastoral Care and Mentoring, Pillar Network; author, *40 Questions about Pastoral Ministry* and *Shepherding the Pastor*

"You don't have to be a member of a local church for many Sundays before you discover that the people in the pews around you can be challenging. Their social media posts make you cringe, their parenting choices make you concerned, and their personalities sometimes just rub you the wrong way. (Of course, you almost certainly do the same to them!) Jamie Dunlop's book is a lifeline for those days when you question whether you're in the right place on Sunday morning. As I read, I was both encouraged and convicted that loving the people in my local church just might be the most radical testimony of Christ that I could make in this world. Whether you are a church member or a church leader, Dunlop's robust theology, practical application, and warm tone will help you push beyond personal comfort toward displaying the glorious name of Jesus. I highly commend it."

Megan Hill, pastor's wife; author, *A Place to Belong*; Managing Editor, The Gospel Coalition

"The world is infatuated with the idea of love but hates its biblical implications. We love for selfish reasons, and want to love when it's convenient. Loving unlovable people is countercultural and, in the world's eyes, scandalous. That's what makes the church unique, because people who have no business getting along selflessly seek each other's good. In *Love the Ones Who Drive You Crazy,* Jamie Dunlop calls us to obey the commands of Scripture and follow our Lord's example to selflessly and sacrificially love one another and pursue unity in diversity."

Chopo Mwanza, Pastor, Faith Baptist Church Riverside, Kitwe, Zambia

Love the Ones Who Drive You Crazy

Eight Truths for Pursuing Unity in Your Church

Jamie Dunlop

CROSSWAY®

WHEATON, ILLINOIS

Library of Congress Cataloging-in-Publication Data

Names: Dunlop, Jamie, author.
Title: Love the ones who drive you crazy : eight truths for pursuing unity in your church / Jamie Dunlop.
Description: Wheaton, Illinois : Crossway, 2023. | Series: 9marks |
Includes bibliographical references and index.
Identifiers: LCCN 2023002733 (print) | ISBN 9781433589928 (trade paperback) | ISBN
 9781433589935 (pdf) | ISBN 9781433589959 (epub)
Subjects: LCSH: Love—Religious aspects—Christianity. | Friendship—Religious aspects—Christianity. |
 Conflict management—Religious aspects—Christianity.
Classification: LCC BV4639 .D856 2023 (print) | LCC BV4639 (ebook) | DDC 231/.6—dc23/
 eng/20230524
LC record available at https://lccn.loc.gov/2023002733
LC ebook record available at https://lccn.loc.gov/2023002734

Crossway is a publishing ministry of Good News Publishers.

BP			32	31	30	29	28	27	26	25	24	23
15	14	13	12	11	10	9	8	7	6	5	4	3	2	1

Contents

Series Preface

THE 9MARKS SERIES of books is premised on two basic ideas. First, the local church is far more important to the Christian life than many Christians today perhaps realize.

Second, local churches grow in life and vitality as they organize their lives around God's Word. God speaks. Churches should listen and follow. It's that simple. When a church listens and follows, it begins to look like the One it is following. It reflects his love and holiness. It displays his glory. A church will look like him as it listens to him.

So our basic message to churches is, don't look to the best business practices or the latest styles; look to God. Start by listening to God's Word again.

Out of this overall project comes the 9Marks series of books. Some target pastors. Some target church members. Hopefully all will combine careful biblical examination, theological reflection, cultural consideration, corporate application, and even a bit of individual exhortation. The best Christian books are always both theological and practical.

It is our prayer that God will use this volume and the others to help prepare his bride, the church, with radiance and splendor for the day of his coming.

Acknowledgments

WITH THANKS TO Isaac Adams for his encouragement to put these ideas into writing; to John Lee, Joan Dunlop, Caleb Morell, Andy Winn, Bobby Jamieson, Ben Lacey, Serennah Harding, Tiago Oliveira, and Joey Craft for their thoughtful feedback on the manuscript; to Jonathan Leeman and Alex Duke at 9Marks and Tara Davis at Crossway for helping this book to take shape; to those who have graciously allowed me to tell their stories; to the congregation at the Capitol Hill Baptist Church for providing me with time to write and for loving me with the love of Christ.

So *This* Is What "Christ Alone" Means?

Conflict in Your Church as Evidence of Faith

If you love those who love you, what benefit is that
to you? For even sinners love those who love them.

LUKE 6:32

The Difficulty of a "Christ Alone" Church

Who isn't discouraged by conflict at church? After all, the local church should be as close as we get to heaven on earth, right? Yet there are so many opportunities for disagreement at church. Conflict comes from differences of opinion, like whether church leaders were right to reduce support for the crisis pregnancy center you love. It comes from differences of conviction, like that church member whose social media feed promotes positions you find morally troubling. Sometimes it's differences of culture or class that make you feel like an outsider in your own church. And sometimes it's no deeper than people who rub you the wrong way.

In fact, I'm convinced that churches are *especially* ripe for conflict, precisely because they should be centered on Christ alone. Think about that for a moment: a church should be defined by Christ alone. Not by Christ *and* shared convictions about children's schooling options, or by Christ *and* an antipoverty strategy, or by Christ *and* shared revulsion at so-and-so's social media post, or by Christ *and* a particular musical vibe. . . . You get the picture. It's easy to *say* the church should be centered on Christ alone. Well, dear reader, living with all these differences and disagreements is what it looks like. And too often we're entirely unprepared for this "Christ alone" kind of a church.

The Glory of a "Christ Alone" Church

Yet the differences and disagreements that threaten to tear your church apart are filled with potential to proclaim the glory of our good and gracious God. That's the burden of this book. After all, the churches of the New Testament were filled with differences and disagreements, just like yours and mine. They emerged from their own culture wars (Jew and Gentile). They came from opposite ends of society (slave and free, rich and poor). They arrived at opposing moral convictions (drinking wine, eating meat). In the New Testament, these disagreements weren't all resolved, and these differences weren't all repudiated. Yet through them and in part *because* of them, God answered Jesus's prayer for unity in John 17 in a powerful way: "That they may become perfectly one, so that the world may know that you sent me and loved them even as you loved me" (John 17:23). For these first Christians, love amidst differences and disagreements revealed the power of being united in Christ alone. And the same is true for you and your church.

This book was written to help you love the people in your church whom you struggle to love because of your differences with them. Sometimes differences at church will be about big issues where the gospel's at stake—like whether a Christian can legitimately pursue a gay lifestyle or whether Christ is the only way to God. In those cases, you should fight for biblical truth even at the cost of unity. Other times, differences won't immediately threaten the gospel, but they'll be significant enough that you and these other Christians need to part ways and go to different churches, trusting God's purposes for that separation just like Paul and Barnabas did at the end of Acts 15. Historic differences over baptism come to mind. Sometimes differences with other members or church leaders will have so damaged your trust in them that you need to leave your church.

This book isn't about any of these church-separating situations, though they are difficult. Instead, this book is for the many situations when you decide that you can stay in your church *despite* all the differences. This book is about building beautiful, Christ-exalting unity when you choose to stay and when you choose to love even the ones who drive you crazy. Keep in mind, of course, that the people in your church who drive you crazy might have similar questions about how to love you!

I'm writing in the years following a time of great turmoil in countless churches—including mine—over issues like race and politics and pandemic precautions. I hear from many Christians that they're looking forward to getting back to times when church can be less complicated. But I'm writing this book because, for a variety of factors (which I'll get to), I doubt we're going back to those days when church felt like a lazy stroll on a summer evening (at least, comparatively speaking). And if we care about the glory of Jesus, that could be a very good thing.

Waves of Conflict

To provide an example of what I mean, let me tell you about the past couple of years at my church in Washington, DC, located a few blocks from the United States Capitol. Tension seemed to come in waves, with each new wave crashing down before the previous one had yet receded. Perhaps you can relate.

Wave 1: In response to a pandemic-related government order, my church stopped meeting in the spring of 2020. Then we began meeting again, outdoors, in a neighboring jurisdiction, since large religious gatherings were outlawed in our city. Neither of these decisions escaped controversy within my church.

Wave 2: In June, our city erupted in protest after the killings of several unarmed Black men and women by police. And my church erupted too. Some members marched in protests. Others were appalled at some of what those protests stood for. On both sides, many felt our church leaders spoke too timidly.

Wave 3: In September, my church voted to bring a lawsuit against our city because of its prohibition against our church meeting outdoors (wave 1 again). Some church members couldn't believe we would work through the courts rather than simply disobey the law. Others felt a lawsuit was way out of line. Meanwhile, wave 2 continued.

Wave 4: In November, our nation held a presidential election between Donald Trump and Joe Biden. Given our location, we're accustomed to this once-every-four-years test of our unity in Christ. People still talk about the day when the Senate majority leader threatened on the morning talk shows to strip a recalcitrant senator of his committee posts—yet both men showed up at our church together—with the sound system run that morning by the assistant to the vice president (from the opposing political party). We have a long history of putting aside political differences under Christ. But this one was different. Convictions were heightened along multiple dimensions. And tension didn't ease with Election Day as many (including some in my church) disputed the official result while others (including some in my church) were aghast at what they saw as societal sabotage. Even praying publicly for the president-elect became a political statement.

The waves continued. In April of 2021, as a result of our lawsuit, we negotiated a return to our church building. Many in the congregation were dismayed that this hadn't happened months earlier, and their pain was on full display. Others were appalled at how callous some in their own church seemed to a pandemic that by then had killed so many, including some they loved.

As one of their pastors, I watched over this restive flock through these seasons of pain. Yet as I had conversation after conversation with unhappy members of my church, I began to see these conflicts less as evidence of failure and more as evidence of faith.

Failure or Faith?

How could all this disagreement be anything other than failure? Isn't church supposed to provide safe harbor from storms of controversy in the world outside? To be sure, my church failed—in many ways—in how we disagreed. Yet at the same time I can describe this turmoil as evidence of faith because nearly all these people continued loving one another despite these differences. What's more, many friendships between would-be enemies became that much richer.

Very often, the existence of disagreement in a church is not a sign that things have gone tragically *wrong*, but that things have gone gloriously *right*. I realize this may sound naïve, but give me a few paragraphs to explain myself. As I noted earlier, a church should be centered on Christ alone. Not on Christ *and* shared opinions about navigating a pandemic *and* the best way to confront racism *and* common political convictions. Some disagreements that rock our world have no place in the church, because Scripture comes down clearly on one side. Yet for the many differences on which Christians can legitimately disagree, controversy in society will often bleed into the church— *if*, that is, we're united around Christ alone. If everyone agreed on all these matters, church would be a lot easier. But easy love rarely shows off gospel power.

This matters because Scripture teaches that unity in Christ despite our differences is a primary way God intends to show off his goodness and glory. Take Romans 15 as an example. After a lengthy section on how Jew and Gentile can live together in the local church despite all their differences, Paul gives this word of blessing:

> May the God of endurance and encouragement grant you to live
> in such harmony with one another, in accord with Christ Jesus,
> that together you may with one voice glorify the God and Father

of our Lord Jesus Christ. Therefore welcome one another as Christ has welcomed you, for the glory of God. (Rom. 15:5–7)

Twice in this short passage, we see God getting glory through the harmony that comes as Christians live *in accord with Christ*. Not that this is easy; note that Paul prays to "the God of endurance and encouragement." Yet if this difficulty had led the first Roman churches to abandon unity, or to insist on uniformity rather than Jew-Gentile diversity, Paul's prayer would have fallen flat. The differences that threaten to tear your church apart are *opportunities* to demonstrate that being "in accord with Christ Jesus" is all we need to be in "harmony with one another." That's how "with one voice" we "glorify the God and Father of our Lord Jesus Christ." If your church is about Jesus *and* immigration reform, you rob him of glory. If your church is about Jesus *and* homeschooling, you rob him of glory. Just as God gets greater glory through redemption than through creation alone, the glory he receives in your church's unity is greater in disagreement and difference than if everyone were in the same place to begin with.

Yet This Is Hard

But living this out is not for the faint of heart. If your church is built on Christ alone, then:

- People in your church won't "get it" on issues that are important to you. "She thinks that if I took the Bible seriously, I'd never own a gun. Can you believe that?"
- Church leaders won't "get it" on issues that are important to you. Your pastors should be careful how they speak on

important issues about which Christians in your church can legitimately disagree—no matter their own opinions. That can make you feel like your church is failing to speak prophetically. "This is the greatest moment of racial reckoning in a generation, and my pastor's just talking about the same old stuff!"

- People in your church won't understand you. You'll find yourself at church with people who lack the similarity in background, opinion, and culture that would allow them to understand you without having to ask. "If one more person asks what it's like having hair like mine, I swear I'm out of here."

- Your church won't be insulated from society's controversies. "I thought that of all places, church would have been the one place where no one would bring up the election."

Too many of us have never really grappled with the implications of a church centered on Christ alone. We applaud diversity in our churches and pray for more diversity, never contemplating the cost and challenge that comes when God answers our prayer.[1]

Consumerism at Church Makes This Harder

What's more, the way many of us have been taught to think about church complicates matters further. Consider for a moment the questions people ask when they're looking for a new church. "Do

---

1 In general, when I speak of "diversity" in this book, I am referring to much more than ethnic or racial diversity. Rather, I'm referring to all the various kinds of differences that exist in a church, which I summarized in the first section of this introduction—including ethnic and racial diversity.

I like their style of music?" "Would I fit into their small groups?" "Will my kids enjoy their children's ministry?" "Do they have a service team for me?" We shop for a church like we shop for a car. "Does it fit my needs? Is it going to give me any trouble? Will it make me look good?" Put simply, we approach church as consumers.

But here's the catch: if you view church as a consumer, what will you do with the very *un*consumer-like traits of churches that are full of people who think differently than you, who don't understand you, and who make you uncomfortable? If you pick a church like you pick a car, what happens when the real cost of Christ-alone diversity becomes apparent? Sometimes, churches are a step ahead of us, designing small groups, church services, or even entire congregations to fit one specific type of person so that these questions rarely confront their members. But that's uniformity, not unity.

Add to that a very modern tendency to want to solve problems rather than live with them (assuming we view these uncomfortable disagreements as "problems") and a general bent toward comfort, and we have a recipe for some serious dissatisfaction with church. At least, that is, with a church centered on Christ alone.

And It's Getting Harder

That's not all. In today's world, several trends are making these challenges progressively more difficult.

Take social media, for example. Despite its potential for good, social media is a real challenge to unity in a diverse church because it advertises our opinions. Think about church in the early 2000s. If you had a particularly edgy opinion about race relations or alternative medicine or gentrification, it came up at church when you wanted it to come up. Today, what would once have surfaced only in private conversation is often posted for public consumption. Which pastor *hasn't* fielded calls from church members who are outraged that a church member could post this or "like" that? What's more, the economics of social media tend toward the edgy, controversial, and sharply-stated. And social media doesn't simply advertise our opinions; it often shapes them. It can even result in different church members coming to different convictions because they're looking at different sets of facts.

Another factor: in the United States, evangelical churches over the past several decades have been increasing in their ethnic and racial diversity.[2] For example, over the past twenty years, the portion of American evangelicals in multiracial churches has doubled[3] while the portion in completely White or completely Black churches fell by more than half.[4] As of 2019, the average congregation is more than twice as diverse along ethnic and racial lines as it was twenty years earlier.[5] This data comes with a host of caveats, especially for those who would take increasing

---

2 From Duke University's National Congregations Study, conducted every five to eight years. The results cited in this paragraph were published in Kevin D. Dougherty, Mark Chaves, and Michael O. Emerson, "Racial Diversity in U.S. Congregations, 1998–2019," *Journal for the Scientific Study of Religion* 59, no. 4 (2020): 551–62.

3 The study defines "multiracial churches" as congregations where no racial group constitutes more than 80 percent of the congregation's participants. In 2018–2019, such congregations accounted for 24 percent of the total, up from 13 percent in 1998.

4 The study reported that it did not have sufficient numbers of completely Asian or completely Hispanic congregations in its dataset to evaluate similar trends for these types of congregations.

5 Note that all three of the trends cited have been observed in every period of study, including the most recent (2012–2019).

diversity as assurance that ethnic and racial tension is behind us.[6] Yet one reality is clear: American evangelicals (particularly if they are White) are far more likely to rub shoulders at church with those of a different ethnicity or race than they were several decades ago. With that comes an increased likelihood that they'll find differences with others at church regarding the many factors and issues that tend to cluster by race and ethnicity. This answer to many prayers comes with many challenges.

Beyond these two trends, it seems that as society becomes more secular, disagreements at church are increasingly matters of conviction and conscience, not just preference. Gone are the "worship wars" of the 1990s. Now we disagree over what a Christian working for a secular company should say during his office's "pride month" celebration, or whether a Christian can recommend a book by a critical theory scholar. We even disagree over whether Christians can legitimately disagree on issues like these. The question is no longer "Do I *want* to go to a church that has a praise band?" but "Will my conscience *allow* me to go to church with people who add gendered pronouns to their email signatures?" Which concessions are legitimate adaptations to a changing culture and which form an uncrossable line? As a prominent sociologist at the University of Illinois wrote in 2021, "I've been studying religion and religious congregations for 30 years. This is a level of conflict that I've never seen."[7] With morality receding in the wider culture like an ebbing tide, Christians

---

6   For example, while diversity has increased as racial minorities have joined majority-White churches, there is almost no sign that the reverse is taking place, and even as majority-White churches become more racially and ethnically diverse, they normally retain a White majority and White leadership.

7   Francis Wilkinson, "America's Churches Are Now Polarized, Too," *Bloomberg Quint*, Febraury 21, 2021.

disagree over which moorings to cling to. Perhaps this trend is the cost of staying faithful to Scripture in an increasingly secular world.

A fourth trend, prevalent at least in the United States, is a decreasing tolerance in societal discourse for any deviation from established political orthodoxy. No one would suggest that politics has ever been peaceful. And the present day is not the worst political polarization we've ever seen (let's not forget the American Civil War). But many social commentators have noted that polarization is markedly more strident than in recent generations, whether we're talking about "cancel culture" on the left or the right's concern with identifying "true" conservatives. Social psychologist Jonathan Haidt has located 2009 as a turning point in this regard. Since then, he says, it has become "more hazardous to be seen fraternizing with the enemy or even failing to attack the enemy with sufficient vigor."[8] For a broad subset of the population, a challenge to any individual political position has become a challenge to one's entire worldview—even at church. As such, positions on issues like gun control or reparations for slavery that a few years ago would have been understood as legitimate disagreements among Christians are now seen to be beyond the pale of Christian fellowship. As evangelical scholar Os Guiness has written, "There is only one short and easy step from 'This is the Christian way' to 'There is only one Christian way' to 'Anything different from this way is not Christian' to 'All those who differ from my way are not Christians.'"[9] Social polarization has most certainly found its way into Christ's church.

8   Jonathan Haidt, "Why the Past 10 Years of American Life Have Been Uniquely Stupid," *The Atlantic*, April 2022.

9   Os Guiness, *Fit Bodies Fat Minds: Why Evangelicals Don't Think and What to Do about It* (Grand Rapids, MI: Baker, 1994), 144–45.

All this makes church hard, and increasingly so. It's hard because we've been sold a consumerist vision of church when, in reality, church is quite sacrificial. It's hard because our differences are increasingly on display, and they're increasingly convictional. It's hard because some people in our churches stretch our love to the breaking point. When we speak of church as "family," we have in mind quiet board games by the fireplace. But sometimes church "family" is more akin to shouting matches over who used up all the hot water.

Fight or Flight

What happens in our churches as a result? Too frequently, we resort to our natural instincts: fight or flight. We fight, standing up to the wimpy pastor who's selling out to the agenda of the [insert odious cause here]. Sometimes that instinct is a good one, when the gospel really is at stake. But sometimes all we accomplish are the "dissensions" and "divisions" Paul condemns as "works of the flesh" in Galatians 5:19–21. Pastor Kevin DeYoung states this danger well: "It may be that your pastor is cowardly trying to make everyone happy. That won't work. But it may be that he is trying to wisely shepherd a diverse flock in a way that helps the sheep to focus on Christ and him crucified."[10]

On the other hand, sometimes we give up on the idea of a church centered on Christ alone and flee to another church where we won't find as much difference, or to no church at all.[11]

---

10 Kevin DeYoung, "What Are We Arguing About?," *DeYoung, Restless, and Reformed* (blog), *The Gospel Coalition*, September 10, 2020, https://www.thegospelcoalition.org/.

11 According to Harvard University's annual Cooperative Election Study, 2016–2020 marked the first period since the study began when the *majority* of self-labeled evan-

Sometimes the instinct to flee is also good, when we need to leave if we're to continue growing in Christ. But too often we're merely exchanging the glory of diversity for the comfort of similarity.

Either way, whether we're wrong in our fight or wrong in our flight, people are hurt, pastors quit, Christians give up on church, gospel power remains unproven, and Christ is dishonored.

The Way Forward

So what should we do? How can we keep loving "those" people in our churches who drive us crazy? Should we avoid them? Confront them? Fight? Flee?

In short, we must *love* them. And to see how, let's begin with some famous words of Jesus: "If you love those who love you, what benefit is that to you? For even sinners love those who love them. . . . But love your enemies . . . and your reward will be great, and you will be sons of the Most High, for he is kind to the ungrateful and the evil. Be merciful, even as your Father is merciful" (Luke 6:32–36).[12] While "those" people in your church are not your enemies—praise God you are one in Christ—they certainly fall toward the "more difficult" end of the spectrum that Jesus lays out. Love them, Jesus says, because God will reward you when you do. And love them so that your mercy will reflect and display God's own enemy-loving mercy, just as a son reflects his father.

---

gelical Christians in the United States did not normally attend a church service on a weekly basis, a trend that was in place long before the COVID-19 pandemic.

12 Jesus isn't merely telling us to love one group of people, our enemies. He's defining a whole ethic of love by staking out its extreme (love even our enemies) to show that easy love is not the love that testifies to God's power. For more on this idea that Jesus is using the command to love your enemies to define an ethic of love, read the opening chapters of D. A. Carson's *Love in Hard Places* (Wheaton, IL: Crossway, 2002).

According to Jesus, it's *this* end of the spectrum—love that's difficult—that matters the most. Just as a tiny set of dumbbells hardly shows off the strength of the bodybuilder, love in your church that's natural and effortless hardly shows off the glory of the gospel that God has worked into your heart. Love that's difficult is the antidote to hypocrisy in the church; it reveals who's really following Jesus and who's just along for the ride (1 John 3:16–18).

Of course, as much as unity amidst difference may be costly to us, it was infinitely more costly to Christ. Consider that the one speaking these words in Luke 6 knew that the mercy he proclaimed would cost him his life. You and I were "evil and ungrateful." Yet he delighted to show us the riches of his mercy. Is that not the Savior we want to proclaim? It is only because his body hung on a cross that we can be members of his body. And his sacrifice was costly enough to pay the price of your church's unity, no matter your differences. As such, I'm convinced that somewhere in this brazen command of Jesus is the elixir of life for your church and for mine.

But how exactly can we love this way?

The Rest of This Book

Let me offer a roadmap for where we're going. Most of this book examines some passages near the end of Paul's letter to the Romans, where Paul explains and expands on Jesus's "love your enemies" ethic of Luke 6.[13] In Romans 12, 14, and 15, Paul addresses a group of churches in Rome who, while united in Christ,

13 While the breadth of these chapters in Romans certainly goes beyond the commands of Luke 6, scholars have noted many thematic links between these two sections of Scripture. Especially given that Luke was Paul's traveling companion, it makes one

were riven with cultural and convictional differences.[14] The result is a gospel-infused blueprint for building genuine, affectionate, and God-glorifying friendships with the people at church who drive you crazy.

Yet Paul doesn't merely give us a list of "how-to" commands. Rather, he reaches behind the commands to describe a set of perspectives that shine a different light on relationships at church. We're accustomed to having our perspectives adjusted by the experiences of those we love. For example, you'll have more sympathy and grace for those struggling with mental illness once your best friend finds herself there. These perspectives Paul gives us do much the same, but at a deeper, more theological level. As such, each chapter in this book examines a different truth that offers a new perspective on those at church you struggle to love. My prayer is that with each new angle, the grip of self-righteousness and complacency on your heart will progressively loosen, investing your love with renewed power, persistence, and joy. In Ephesians 4:3, Paul tells us to be "eager to maintain the unity of the Spirit in the bond of peace." You might think of these chapters as a guide to maintaining God-given unity in your church, and how to do so eagerly.

---

wonder how much common source material or connection there may have been in the writing of these two books of the Bible, with Romans most likely written first.

14 Why will we skip Romans 13? Because chapter 13 is really a parenthesis, an excursus in the middle of Paul's teaching on love. As Paul delves into the topic of love, he encourages us at the end of chapter 12 to "never avenge yourselves, but leave it to the wrath of God" (12:19). That raises the question whether we should ever pursue earthly justice. Romans 13 is Paul's answer: earthly government has been instituted by God to pursue earthly justice. Then, in the closing verses of chapter 13, Paul transitions back to his main theme of love in the church, which he continues through chapter 14 and the beginning of chapter 15.

A Critical Assumption

Of course, that phrase "the unity *of the Spirit*" is an important one. If your congregation has many people in it who aren't indwelt by the Spirit of God because they haven't been born again, this book will likely be more frustrating than helpful. This is a book about pursuing unity in Christ, but it assumes that the ones who drive you crazy in your church are in fact *in Christ*; that is, people who have turned away from their sin in order to follow Christ, trusting in him alone for salvation, and have received God's supernatural gift of regeneration, of being born again (John 3:3–5).

This isn't the same as saying that everyone present at your Sunday service is a Christian; I would hope that there are dozens or even hundreds of self-conscious unbelievers attending your church because they want to give the gospel a hearing. But I *am* assuming that the members of your church can give a credible profession of faith so that, while only God can know who is truly born again, there is good reason to believe that they are at least largely regenerate.[15] If your church is *not* united in Christ, then this book is premature. I pray that you will see this change over time as the true gospel is preached and believed. But seeking to implement the principles of this book in a church full of non-Christians will merely result in frustration and confusion.

---

15 For some churches, what I am describing is what our theological forebearers termed "regenerate church membership." For churches that practice infant baptism, what I have in mind is a regenerate communing membership. In this paragraph I use the term "largely regenerate" because in no church can we ever be fully confident that every member (or communing member) is a Christian. Jesus warned us of our human tendency toward self-deception (Matt. 7:22–23); that is why Jesus gave us the tool of church discipline (Matt.18:15–20). For more on this matter, see chapters 1–2 in *The Compelling Community* by Mark Dever and Jamie Dunlop (Wheaton, IL: Crossway, 2015).

Why All These Differences?

On the other hand, love for one another in a church that *is* composed of Christians—despite their differences—is a beautiful testimony to the power of the gospel. This is where the rest of this book will focus. Yet first we must undertake some important groundwork. Very often, we're inclined to think that all the debate and disagreement in a church is a giant distraction from its mission. "If we could all just get along, then we could get back to what our church is supposed to be doing." Yet as we see in Luke 6, and later in Romans, all this disagreement and debate isn't distraction at all. It's center stage for the *ultimate* mission of your church: to show off the goodness and glory of God Most High.

But this message will ring hollow if, like many evangelicals, we've reduced the purpose of the church to the things it does, like community and missions and evangelism. If church matters merely for what it *does*, then we'll find little patience for all the differences and disagreements I've described. On the other hand, once we discover God's true calling for a church, to be a display of his glory (which encompasses the things it does and much more), then the motivations Scripture gives us suddenly come alive. It's to that topic—the purpose of your church—that we now turn.

Questions for Reflection and Discussion

1. What kinds of people in your church do you struggle to love (e.g., people who don't understand your cultural background, people who think differently on politics, people whose personalities clash with yours, etc.)?

2. In what ways have you seen differences between congregants in your church become more pronounced in recent years?

3. Reread Romans 15:5–7. In your church, what kinds of harmony glorify God?

Prayer Points

- Pray that your desire to love those in your church whom you find to be difficult would grow.
- Pray that your fellow church members would cherish God-honoring unity in your church.
- Pray for the leaders of your church to accurately discern which divisions in your congregation threaten gospel unity.

1

Why Did God Put Difficult People in My Church?

Truth 1: Insistence on Unity
Displays the Glory of God

May the God of endurance and encouragement grant
you to live in such harmony with one another, in accord
with Christ Jesus, that together you may with one voice
glorify the God and Father of our Lord Jesus Christ.

ROMANS 15:5–6

When Unity Costs Too Much

Trinity Church was in trouble. And its trouble sprang from what had only recently seemed to be its great strength. Like many urban congregations, the church had steadily declined for years until only the old stalwarts remained. Then young people started moving into the neighborhood, many attending Trinity. The newly multigenerational congregation delighted in its diversity.

That is, until now. As the young newcomers shifted from a welcomed minority to a new majority, Trinity was waking up to a wild new level of disagreement in its pews. The old guard who had prided themselves on folding younger members into leadership were becoming resentful of the direction those new leaders were taking them. Younger members felt that their seniors were slow to adapt to a changing neighborhood. Budget meetings were exceedingly difficult, with newer members wanting more family ministry and older members wanting to recapture the church's historical commitment to international work. The pastor was regularly scolded by older and younger members alike for sermon application that seemed too targeted toward the needs of the other group. Picking songs was a tightrope act.

As much as everyone hated to admit it, Trinity was divided. What's more, division was stifling mission. The team who'd faithfully volunteered for years at the local homeless shelter disbanded, complaining of a "takeover" by younger volunteers who wanted more focus on addiction recovery. A group of younger church members informed the elders they would no longer contribute to the missions fund until longstanding missionaries were reevaluated. Giving to the general fund was down by almost a third, a reflection of frustration by older and younger members alike.

"This is ridiculous," the pastor exclaimed in frustration. "How have we gone from happily serving together one year to an embarrassing catfight the next? After all, why are we here? Missions? Well, clearly that's suffering. Evangelism? Who wants to come to a church like this? Spiritual growth? All this division is just slowing us down." In desperation, he floated a solution to the leadership team. "Look," he said, "we've been saving up to build a bigger sanctuary. What if, instead, we use that money to buy another building and just divide into two churches? After all, that's what we've really become. Then we can spend our time serving Jesus instead of fighting."

What's the Purpose of a Church?

What do you think? Is the pastor's solution a wise recognition of reality? Or an unfortunate retreat? That depends largely on how you answer his question, "Why are we here?" My guess is that if you were to ask the average member of Trinity what the purpose of their church is, you'd get one of two answers (or both). One answer has to do with what Trinity Church can do for *God*. Things like international missions, church planting, mercy ministry, and so forth. The other answer has to do with what the church does for *them*. Things like building community, helping them grow in faith, teaching their kids about Jesus, and providing opportunities to serve. But like Trinity was discovering, an insistence on unity given all their differences was confounding both aims. On the surface, it would appear this pastor is on to something. Like Paul and Barnabas, perhaps they should go their separate ways so they can stop fighting, work hard for Jesus, and figure the rest out in heaven.

Churches *Designed* to Explode?

Yet I would maintain that this mindset runs counter to the New Testament's priorities for church. Here's what I mean. Imagine that you were a first-century Christian in Rome. Knowing that

Jew and Gentile mix together as well as oil and water, you'd have one church for Jews and another for Gentiles. One strategy for reaching Jews and another for Gentiles. At least, that's what makes sense to me. But as Scripture makes quite clear, God's plan for these churches was to be Jew-Gentile from the very beginning, with all the miscommunication, mistrust, and misunderstanding that no doubt ensued. It was an explosive combination.

In fact, the churches of the New Testament were often built of combustible materials. The first church, we discover in Acts 6, was both Hebrew *and* Hellenist, Jews from different cultures famous for their mutual animosity.[1] The church in Colossae was both slave *and* free. The church in Corinth had people who ate meat sacrificed to idols *and* those who thought that was sin. The churches James wrote to were rich *and* poor. Differences of culture, differences of conscience, differences of class. Some explosive material!

I'll bet your church is a bit of a tinderbox too. Your divisions may not be generational like Trinity's, but surely there are fault lines that run through your congregation. Just think of all the possible disagreements: how to apply biblical teaching on gender, what music to sing, how to run the children's ministry, how to navigate a world enamored with the LGBTQ agenda. Not to mention more theological disagreements. Not to mention ordinary, run-of-the-mill church disagreements like what to prioritize in the budget and what color to put on the walls. And those are just in the category of disagreements. What about differences of culture, personality, social strata, and—I'm sure—three or four categories

---

1   K. C. Hanson and Douglas E. Oakman, *Palestine in the Time of Jesus: Social Structures and Social Conflicts* (Minneapolis: Augsburg Fortress, 1998), 149.

that immediately jump to your mind I haven't thought to mention? Like the churches of the New Testament, your insistence on unity amidst difference means that the explosives are set, the switch is set to "hair trigger," and the fireworks are ready to go. So why not simply become two (or more) happier, more productive, more homogeneous churches?

Challenging the Utilitarian View of Church

To answer that, let's revisit the question Trinity's pastor was asking: "Why are we here?" Or, stated more precisely, "What's the purpose of a local church?" I suggested two answers: doing things for God, or doing things for us. While both answers are true, they're incomplete. Why? In part, because neither can explain the New Testament's clear enthusiasm for churches that find unity amidst great difference. If we want to have patience and enthusiasm to love those in our churches who drive us crazy, we must find in the Scriptures a deeper purpose statement for church.

To begin, note that the two answers I gave to the question "Why are we here" are rather utilitarian in nature. They're focused on what a church produces. They value church based on what it produces for *us* (community, teaching, etc.) or for *God* and for *others* (international missions, mercy ministry, etc.). However, as I'll explain in a few paragraphs, God's purpose for a church isn't found merely in its *utility* but in its *beauty*. Not simply in *production* but in *reflection*; that is, in reflecting who God is as a display of his glory. If we can recover the biblical priority of the local church as a reflection of God's glory—and beyond that, the pleasure and power of reflecting his glory—we will recover new appreciation, patience, perspective, and even enthusiasm for love that's hard. To show you this from Scripture, let me take you on a brief tour of the idea of "beautiful reflection," from Eden to Israel, from Jesus to the church.

Beautiful Reflection: The Story Begins

This story begins in Genesis 1, when "God created man in his own image, / in the image of God he created him; / male and female he created them" (Gen. 1:27). The purpose of human beings is rooted in our unique status as those made in his image. Our nature is our job description: to reflect the glory of who God is, just as your image in the mirror reflects who you are. Then, having created mankind, God "blessed" them (Gen. 1:28). When God "blesses" in Genesis, be it the animals (1:22), the Sabbath (2:3), or Noah (9:1), he's explaining how his purposes for each aspect of creation will be accomplished.[2] Here's our blessing: "Be fruitful and multiply and fill the earth and subdue it, and have dominion over the fish of the sea and over the birds of the heavens and over every living thing that moves on the earth" (Gen. 1:28). Putting these pieces together: we will reflect who God is (Gen. 1:27) as we rule God's creation as his representatives and as we fill the earth with a society of those made in his image (Gen. 1:28).

Do you see the relationship between doing things for God and reflecting who God is? We're made according to his image, and our life's purpose is to advertise how good and amazing he

---

2 Regarding God's blessing on Abraham, Peter Gentry and Stephen Wellum note: "Blessings are the manifestation of a faithfulness, fidelity, and solidarity in relationships whereby one's natural and personal capacity to fulfill God's intention and purpose is advanced and furthered" *Kingdom through Covenant* (Wheaton, IL: Crossway, 2012), 278.

is (Gen. 1:27). We *live that out* through our labor and our love, through our rule and our relationships, as described in Genesis 1:28. As such, you are less like a machine, designed to do things for God, and more like a beautiful painting, created to display his glory.

After all, God didn't create us because he needed us to do things for him. He was ruling the earth just fine before we came along. In his creative genius, he was filling the earth just fine. Instead, his primary purpose for you and for me is to display the glory of who he is. Production serves reflection.

When we look for meaning in the things we do (production) absent what those actions say about God (reflection), we get into trouble. Consider, for instance, how the idols of our world correspond so well with God's commands in Genesis 1:28. The idolatry of power (be it your work or your money) finds meaning for life in God's command to exercise dominion. The idolatry of love finds meaning in relationships, something quite integral to God's command to be fruitful and to fill the earth. It's no wonder then, that in Genesis 3 God curses these very things—exercising dominion (3:17), relationships, and fruitfulness (3:16)—so that we will never succeed in our quest to find purpose in what we do, divorced from our deeper purpose of reflecting the glory of our Creator.

The Story Continues: Israel to the New Creation

Fast-forward past the creation account. Through the patriarchs, God creates an entire nation and, once again, his purpose for them is reflective in nature. We can sum up the laws and regulations that fill the early books of the Bible in a phrase: "Be holy, for I am holy." (Lev. 11:44). What's more, reflection was to be evangelistic, pointing "the peoples" to the glory of Israel's God (Deut. 4:6–7).

But that's not what Old Testament Israel did. They worshiped idols instead. More specifically: Ashtoreth, the goddess of fertility (idolizing fruitfulness), and Baal, the god of storm and rain, and therefore of good harvests, who ruled the divine pantheon (idolizing work and rule).[3] Like us, they idolized Genesis 1:28 (rule and fill), divorced from Genesis 1:27 (made in God's image). Rather than leading lives of worship as those made in God's image, Israel worshiped images of what God had cursed.

In fact, that use of the word *image* brings up an important point. For the first nine chapters of Genesis, *image* is a positive concept. "God created man in his own image." But from Genesis 10 through Malachi, the word takes on a universally negative connotation, describing the graven images people worship instead of God. It's astonishing, really, that such a foundational term in the Old Testament's opening chapters is never again used in a positive sense. It's as if the Old Testament were begging for the New.

Sure enough, as we enter the New Testament, *image* is once again a positive term. But who does it refer to now? "Christ, who is the image of God" (2 Cor. 4:4). "He is the image of the invisible God, the firstborn of all creation" (Col. 1:15). One significant way in which Christ succeeded where Adam failed is that he, finally, is the perfect image of God.[4] As Jesus says to Philip in John 14:9, "Whoever has seen me has seen the Father."

---

3 Mark S. Smith, *The Early History of God: Yahweh and the Other Deities in Ancient Israel* (Grand Rapids, MI: Eerdmens, 2002), 68.

4 Note that Christ is more than just a perfect Adam. Whereas Adam and Eve were made "according to" God's image, Christ *is* the image of God.

Yet this story of reflection does not end with Jesus. Jesus came to save a people for himself whom God "predestined to be conformed to the image of his Son" (Rom. 8:29). As men and women who are being recreated in Christ, we reflect the glory of God not merely individually but corporately. Jesus said it's our love "for one another" that marks us off as his disciples (John 13:35). Beyond that, love despite differences makes a particularly powerful statement about the worth of Christ. Thus Paul's repeated image of the church as the body of Christ, representing him in a multiplicity of backgrounds (Eph. 4:16; 1 Cor. 12:13) and gifts (Rom. 12:5–6; 1 Cor. 12:27–28). Paul writes that unity between Jew and Gentile shows off his wisdom even to the heavenly beings (Eph. 3:8, 10). And he tells the Colossians to relate to each other in love because they "have put on the new self, which is being renewed in knowledge after the image of its creator. Here there is not Greek and Jew, circumcised and uncircumcised, barbarian, Scythian, slave, free; but Christ is all, and in all" (Col. 3:10–11). Love amidst difference was a key aspect of how these Christians would represent the image of God.

When a church in all its differences unites around Jesus, it reflects the wisdom and power and glory of God far beyond what we can do as individuals. As a nineteenth-century pastor wrote, "The Church is the mirror, that reflects the whole effulgence of the Divine character. It is the grand scene, in which the perfections of Jehovah are displayed to the universe."[5]

Where does this story end? With reflection and the reflected one joining together. In Revelation 21:10–11, we behold the

5   Charles Bridges, *The Christian Ministry, with an Inquiry into the Causes of Its Inefficiency* (Edinburgh: Banner of Truth Trust, 2005), 1.

bride of the Lamb, the church, who is "the holy city Jerusalem coming down out of heaven from God, having the glory of God." What does it mean that this city *has* the glory of God? Is this reflection, where the glory of the city displays the glory of God? Or is it the reflected one, God, who dwells there (Rev. 21:3)? Now that faith has become sight, it's both. The kings of the earth bring the glory of the nations into the city (Rev. 21:24), and the glory of God himself is its light (Rev. 21:23). Throughout human history, God's name has been tarnished, his goodness slandered, his justice mocked. As reflections of his glory, our lives as God's people have argued the truth about him, albeit imperfectly, both as individuals and together. Now at last in Revelation 21, the beauty and glory of the one to whom our lives have pointed is unmistakable.

Let's summarize. Your purpose as a created being, your purpose as a re-created being, and your church's purpose as a community of re-created beings are all one and the same: to reflect the glory and goodness of your Creator. As I noted earlier, you are less of a machine, designed to do things for God, and more of a beautiful painting, created to reflect his glory. The good things that you and your church do are simply the pigments in that painting, the means toward a greater end of reflecting his goodness and glory. This truth has three implications for any church who, like Trinity, struggles with difference and disagreement.

Implication 1: The Priority of Beautiful Reflection

To whatever extent we've located the main purpose of a church in what it produces—either for us or for God—this story of reflection should clarify our thinking. It reminds us that doing good things matters primarily because that's how we show off the glory of our good God. Again, production serves reflection.[6]

My own church struggled with this during the COVID-19 pandemic. With everything shut down, people were frustrated that isolation was impeding discipling, missions, and evangelism, and they were frustrated that so much attention was consumed by the many difficult conversations we were having as a church. I was frustrated too. But I had to remind myself that God's delight is not mainly in how much we produce for him, but in how well we reflect him. Sometimes merely *being* the church shouts great glory to God—because of what unity amidst disagreement and difference proclaims about his sufficiency—even when the things we hope to accomplish seem stalled.

Think of the people in your church you find difficult to love. It would be easy to ignore and avoid them, and even to rationalize doing so. "I don't want to stir up trouble and be a distraction." But what changes your mindset entirely is the realization that your church's *primary* purpose is to reflect the glory of God through unity together. That realization turns people from being obstacles to being treasured.

For example, imagine Rachel, a Jewish Christian in first-century Ephesus who's just about had it with Sophia, her Gentile sister in Christ. Rachel sees Sophia as completely ignorant of ancient Jewish tradition, not having a clue how hard it is for Jews to

6 Consider Paul's teaching in Ephesians 2:9–10. We were saved through faith—not as a result of works (2:9). Why? "For we are his workmanship, created in Christ Jesus for good works" (2:10). The main "work" in view in these verses is not ours but God's. He saved us so we could do good works to show off *his* workmanship, the new creation he has wrought in our hearts. Your good work matters because it shows off God's good work.

invite Gentiles to be full members of the family. "Waltzing into the church like she owns the place!" Not only that, but Sophia feels free to buy anything she finds at the meat market without a thought as to which idol it might have been sacrificed to.

But Rachel has been reading Paul's letter. She knows her feelings of resentment are wrong. So, despite the struggle in her heart, she resists the temptation to avoid Sophia but instead insists on loving her. "God says we're one household of faith, and I'm going to live that way if it kills me!" (see Eph. 2:19). Imagine that what begins awkwardly at first eventually becomes a true friendship. When Paul writes in Ephesians 3:10 that even the rulers and authorities in the heavenly realms stare in wonder at the Ephesian church, it's people like Rachel and Sophia he has in mind. This difficulty, this faith-filled struggle to love, isn't a distraction from the "real" work of ministry; it's the main event! Beyond that, it's the road to joy, which brings us to a second implication of the Bible's story of beautiful reflection.

Implication 2: The Pleasure of Beautiful Reflection

Not long before I wrote this book, a woman named Tabitha was baptized at my church. She had come to believe the Christian gospel by watching religious debates with her atheist father. The more she watched, the more she realized that she agreed with the Christians. Yet this realization filled her with dread. What a terribly inconvenient truth to believe, she thought. "Surely this will destroy my life." But then she found a church. "When I came, it was like stepping into a dreamworld. It took me from begrudgingly acknowledging God to delighting in him." In hindsight, she thinks she truly came to faith when she discovered this delight.

In similar fashion, if God is to be glorified in our churches, we must believe that the beautiful reflection of a church full of differences is not merely important, but delightful. Even if initially we perceive that delight only by faith.

Where does this pleasure come from? It comes as we see Jesus in our relationships with each other, like Tabitha did. You've probably experienced this. You look around at the different members of your church small group and think, "This is crazy! There's no way we'd be friends except for Jesus, and what a friendship we have!" That's the pleasure of beautiful reflection. The slow movement of obedience from the category of "ought to" to the category of "delight to" glorifies the God we serve as good and delightful in all that he does. That's one reason why the term I'm using in this chapter isn't *reflection* but *beautiful reflection*, because our goal in the church is to reflect a Savior who is beautiful, desirable, and satisfying.

The pleasure of reflection also comes as we participate in it ourselves. Let's say you have the chance to help reconcile two brothers in your church who have been at odds. Several months later, you catch sight of them out of the corner of your eye, clearly enjoying each other's company. What a thrill! What's more, your joy at assisting their reconciliation is a shadow of God's joy as the great peacemaker. It's like you're a little kid, jumping from one of your dad's footprints to the next at the beach, imitating God and discovering how delightful it must be for God to be God. That's what turns reflection into worship. As you imitate God in your love for your church, the pleasure you feel reveals new dimensions to how delightful God really is.

Marriage offers an excellent illustration of how all this should work. Is the purpose of marriage to raise children and provide companionship? It is . . . yet to define its purpose merely in terms of what it produces misses the point. For my wife's fortieth birthday, I surprised her with tickets to see the musical *Hamilton* on Broadway. Unbeknownst to me, she'd been longing to go but felt she shouldn't ask because it seemed too extravagant. Her reaction, in the words of my daughter: "Mommy, you squealed!" It was the perfect gift, and it made my wife feel wonderfully known and cherished and loved.

Was this gift worth the cost? Of course! But why? Merely because it helps us to accomplish more with our marriage? Goodness, no! The value of the gift is how it helps us better reflect Christ's love for us, which Paul says in Ephesians 5 is the main point of our marriage. My wife gets to experience how safe and delightful it is to follow one who loves her, which gives us both a better understanding of the privilege we have in following Christ. I get to experience the joy of giving of myself for her good and happiness, which helps us both better understand the joy Jesus has in giving himself for us (Heb. 12:2). To reduce marriage to its outputs is crass and belittling. To value how it reflects the love of Christ without *delighting* in that reflection falls flat. In the same way, God is honored when our churches delight to reflect his perfections through our life together. And as we saw in Luke 6 a few pages back, it's love for those we wouldn't naturally love that makes for an especially delightful and powerful display—which leads to a third implication.

Implication 3: The Power of Beautiful Reflection

Think back to those New Testament churches that seemed destined to explode. Explode they did! But not in division. They were explosive in the power of their gospel witness. The faith of the Romans was reported around the world (Rom. 1:8), and the Jew-Gentile church in Ephesus glorified God's wisdom even to those *outside* this world (Eph. 3:10).

Beautiful reflection is magnificent in its power. In the churches of the New Testament, Jesus's prayer in John 17:21 was coming true: "That they may all be one, just as you, Father, are in me, and I in you, that they also may be in us, so that the world may believe that you have sent me." Reflection ("that they may all be one, just as you, Father, are in me, and I in you") feeds production ("that the world may believe"). There's no "either-or" trade-off between the beauty of a church reflecting Jesus on the one hand, and the good that's done as they proclaim Jesus on the other. How many first-century Christians began their road to belief through the powerful witness of unity between Christian Jews and Christian Gentiles?

Put On Your Faith Glasses

With all this in mind, let's return to Trinity's dilemma. Are they right to split into two churches? That's hard to say. Whatever the right answer, it's clear that they're using the wrong standard to make their decision. They're evaluating ministry success based on what they can accomplish together rather than their ability to portray Christ, as a beautiful, multifaceted reflection of his glory. If the local church can be assessed in terms of its outputs (numbers, baptisms, new churches started, missionaries sent out, etc.), then we'll have little patience for all the disagreements that would distract us from "mission." That's why, if we would love well, we must recover the primary mission of the church as beautiful reflection.

After all, whose life will result in greater glory to God: the brilliant Christian author loved by millions? Or your own version of Euodia and Syntyche (Phil. 4:2), who, in faith, must fight for friendship? In God's economy, how can we know? Yet if it's our *faith* that brings pleasure to God (Heb. 11:6), I suspect we may be surprised at how much of the glory we see in heaven comes from faith-filled strugglers like these two in Philippi. Which chapters in your church's life will result in greater glory to God: times of amazing productivity, or times that took extreme faith just to stay together, showing off Christ's power at work? Who are we to say? Yet there is such a strong impulse in all of us to discount the struggles as unfortunate distraction, when in fact they may be the times when the supremacy of Christ was most loudly proclaimed by your church.

It's like watching a 3-D movie. With your bare eyes, the picture's blurry. But pop those glasses on, and a whole new dimension appears. The beautiful reflection of a church is like 3-D glasses that reveal the dimension of a congregation's faith. Yes, on the surface all we see is dissension, disagreement, and turmoil. But pop those glasses on, and suddenly you can see faith, reflecting back the glory and worthiness and beauty of God. I find it interesting that when Paul begins his letter to the Romans—whose churches were full of potentially explosive differences—he marvels at their *faith* (Rom. 1:8). Paul had his faith glasses on! And so must we.

Recovering the church's purpose, pleasure, and power as a beautiful reflection of Jesus helps us see why we should persevere in love. But how can we do that? What gospel tools does Jesus give us? That's our topic for the remaining pages of this book, as we take inventory of all that Christ has provided in the closing chapters of Paul's letter to the Romans.

Questions for Reflection and Discussion

1. What goes wrong when Christians conceive of a church's purpose merely in terms of the ministry it produces?

2. In your own words, trace the story of beautiful reflection from Genesis to Israel to Jesus to the church.

3. Which of the three implications of this story of beautiful reflection (priority, pleasure, power) is most thought-provoking for you?

Prayer Points

- Pray that your ambitions for your church would increasingly reflect God's ambitions for your church.
- Pray that your congregation would be a beautiful reflection of God and his glory.
- Pray that your church leaders would be patient and hopeful during seasons when your church is less productive than they would like.

2

How Can I Love "Those" People?

Truth 2: Impossible Love Flows
from Impossible Mercy

*I appeal to you therefore, brothers, by the mercies of
God, to present your bodies as a living sacrifice, holy and
acceptable to God, which is your spiritual worship.*

ROMANS 12:1

I Just Can't!

"I can't do this!" "I don't want to!" "You can't make me!"

Are those the words of a whiny child . . . or my own heart as
I contemplate loving the ones who drive me crazy at church? "Of
course I won't be mean, but I'd honestly rather avoid him. Much less
engage him in conversation. Let alone build a *friendship* with him."
Have you ever felt that way? Where can you find the strength, the
generosity, and the warmth, to love "those people" in your church?

Perhaps, like many, you've found inspiration in the story of Corrie ten Boom, who survived the Ravensbruck concentration camp during World War II. In *The Hiding Place*, Corrie famously relates an episode after the war when she was speaking at a church in Munich. A man approached to shake her hand, marveling at the forgiveness of Jesus she'd just described. She recognized him: he was her former jailer.

"His hand was thrust out to shake mine. And I, who had preached so often to the people . . . the need to forgive, kept my hand at my side. Even as angry, vengeful thoughts boiled through me, I saw the sin of them. Jesus Christ had died for this man; was I going to ask for more? . . . I breathed a silent prayer. 'Jesus, I cannot forgive him. Give Your forgiveness.'" And she took the man's hand.

"Then this healing warmth seemed to flood my whole being, bringing tears to my eyes. 'I forgive you, brother!' I cried. 'With all my heart!' For a long moment we grasped each other's hands, the former guard and the former prisoner. I had never known God's love so intensely as I did then."[1]

Of course, you might say, that's the Christian superhero Corrie ten Boom. "Can I really be expected to do the same? Can't I just avoid these people and pretend they don't exist?"

What can you do when you feel like this? Keep in mind that God's standard for love in your church isn't merely that you refrain from saying mean things to "those people." It's not merely that you tolerate them. According to Romans 12:10, God's standard is *brotherly affection* (which we'll get to later in this book). How can you possibly do that?

---

1   Corrie ten Boom, *The Hiding Place* (Bloomington, MN: Chosen Books, 2006), 247–48.

"But That's Impossible" Is the Whole Point

Remember that God often asks his people for the impossible. In Exodus 13–14, God led his people out of slavery in Egypt and into an impossible predicament. They were trapped between the Red Sea ahead and the pursuing army behind. Yet God led them through the sea. I love how Isaiah put it, hundreds of years later:

> Thus says the LORD,
>> who makes a way in the sea,
>> a path in the mighty waters. (Isa. 43:16)

In other words, this is not merely something that God did once upon a time. Making a way through the sea is his signature move!

Jesus tells the man with the withered hand to stretch it out (Matt. 12:13). "But that's impossible!" He tells the crippled man to get up and walk (John 5:8). "But that's impossible!" He tells the dead man to get up (John 11:43). "But that's impossible!" Jesus's commands offer more than instruction; they empower. At his command, the withered hand stretches out. The lame man walks. The dead man walks.

The same is true of life in your church. Easy love rarely shows off gospel power. But love that stretches beyond what's possible is a stage, set to display the glory of God.

The Limits of "Ought To"

"OK," you say. "I'm sold! I love this idea of church as beautiful reflection. I'm going to go build friendships with people in my church who are different from me, where we often disagree and don't share much in common aside from Jesus. And together we're going to show off the power of the gospel!" That determination is a good start, but if that's as far as you go, you're asking for trouble. Before we go any further, we should rope off one potentially harmful route to obedience.

In friendship, real motives become evident over time. "Do you really love me? Or do you love what it *looks like* to love me?" That can smell like tokenism, not friendship. And too many of the brothers and sisters in your church who are accustomed to feeling different from the rest have learned the hard way that they are sometimes valued mainly because they make the church look better. These could be people who are different from most of the church in terms of skin color, social class, age, political leanings, and so forth. I should tread carefully here. I don't want to portray obedience-oriented love as entirely wrongheaded. "Ought to" is an entirely valid reason to love others in your church (John 14:15; 15:12). "Ought to" can be a good starting point for love, but "ought to" cannot be the furthest extent of your ambitions for love. If you love simply because you *ought* to love, then your love may come across as something less than love. And such love loses its luster once its true motivation comes to light.

How can we move from avoiding "those people," to tolerating them, to loving them because we "ought" to, to loving them with affection as family?

Treasure God's Mercy

The answer is mercy. The road from "ought to" to "want to" begins with God's mercy. That's what we see in Romans 12:1: "I appeal to you therefore, brothers, by the mercies of God, to present your bodies as a living sacrifice, holy and acceptable to God, which is your spiritual worship." With this verse, Paul begins one of Scripture's longest discourses on love. But let's not rush into his imperatives so quickly that we skip over what makes such love possible.

"By the mercies of God." In Romans 1–11, the mercies of God have reconciled Jew and Gentile to God through faith in Christ and, as a result, to one other. Then, in Romans 12, we learn the practicalities of this union. It's like Paul is saying, "Congratulations! You're one big happy family (Rom. 1–11). Now let's figure out how this is going to work (Rom. 12–15)." Specifically, the love he will describe in these chapters is a love that's powered by mercy.

What is mercy? Mercy is God rescuing us from the consequences of our sin. That's one reason why we must resist the temptation to minimize or ignore our sin. We often consider the undeserved blessings we've received as Christians (adoption as his sons, the inheritance of heaven, the gift of the Spirit, and many more). But for many, we're less accustomed to considering the punishment Jesus took for us. Yet if we do not comprehend sin's consequences that we should have borne, we will fail to appreciate the wealth of God's mercy in Christ, and our love will be weak.

I remember when this hit home for me. I had gossiped about an acquaintance at church, sharing private information with a group of people. He was understandably embarrassed when he discovered what I'd done, and angry at me for poking fun at something so sensitive. He confronted me, I apologized, and I confessed to God. Ordinarily I would have left things there and moved on.

But this time I decided to take Paul's words seriously. I stared into the sin of my heart. I saw that what masqueraded as a small sin was in fact quite significant. I'd carelessly and selfishly abused this man's trust, getting attention from others at his expense. Not only that, but my sin against Jesus was even greater. The only reason I had this information in the first place was because this man was my brother in Christ, and I had abused Christ's gift of this relationship. When I prioritized a few laughs above this man's dignity, I was devaluing Christ, the source of his dignity. The more I followed my sin down into the recesses of my heart, the worse it appeared, and the more I saw that this sin was primarily against Christ (Ps. 51:4). Far from the "little sin" I'd initially dismissed, it was a big, ugly mess.

Then began the wonderful journey up into the heights of God's mercy. God already knew all this! He knew it all when in his mercy he sent Jesus to die in my place to take the punishment I deserved. He gave me new life, knowing I'd sometimes use it to defame those he'd died for. He loved me *that* much. And in these unexplored depths of God's mercy, I discovered a new degree of love for God. The whole process took maybe five or ten minutes. Yet never since have I viewed confession of sin as a merely perfunctory duty. It's alive with opportunity to behold the mercy of God in all its love-giving power.

Brother or sister, if you are to love the "unlovables" in your church, you must begin to grasp how unlovable *you* were when Christ chose to put his love on you, and how unlovable you remain today even as you are secure in his love. To whatever extent you minimize your sin, or offer excuses for it, or decide not to think about it, you undermine the power of God in your life. On the other hand, when you *do* grasp the astounding truth of God's mercy, it will change everything. In particular, it will change your ability to love, which is where Paul takes us next.

Respond with Sacrificial Love

The churches at Rome were comprised of both Jews and Gentiles, ancient enemies primed for discord yet reconciled in Christ. Paul instructs them to present their bodies (plural) as a living sacrifice (singular). Not many individual sacrifices, not two sacrifices (one Jewish, one Gentile), but one. And as the rest of Romans 12 makes clear, the sacrifice Paul has in mind is a sacrifice of love (see Rom. 12:9)—and especially, love for those they'd otherwise struggle to love (see Rom. 12:16; 14:1).

How exactly does mercy empower sacrificial love? Let's say you're faced with a challenging relationship at church. Perhaps a person is irritating, or clearly doesn't appreciate you, or seems smug and arrogant, or holds opinions you despise. You don't need to agree with him. But you know you must love him! And as with Corrie ten Boom, love has fled your heart, no matter the protestations of your guilty conscience. What can you do? Begin by confessing this very sin, the sin of not loving, just as Corrie did. Turn your mind away from this difficult person and confess your heart's reluctance as what it is: *sin*, as humbling as that might be. Consider how repulsive your sin is to God. Consider the mercy you've received even for this very sin, that in Christ you are forgiven—and at what cost! As knowledge of mercy flows into gratitude, and gratitude into love for God, remember that God has called you to love this person.

There's a saying in my house that's so common, my children have threatened to carve it on my tombstone (which they may yet do): *When you have an attitude problem, it means you have a gratitude problem.* Having lost sight of God's mercy, your heart is deficient in gratitude, and so your love is deficient in power. It's no surprise that two verses later, Paul warns us against pride (Rom. 12:3). Pride blinds us to our sin, which blinds us to God's mercy, which debilitates our love.

And did you notice how Paul describes this sacrificial love in Romans 12:1? "Your spiritual worship." For those of us programmed to think of "worship" merely in terms of music, this phrase seems out of place. Yet it's this word *worship* that brings Paul's teaching into focus. Worship is the right response of created beings to the glory of who God is, a response that can come in song, in word, or in action (action being what Paul primarily has in mind here). Love in the church is worship because it's a beautiful reflection of the one who showed mercy.

All that Paul will command in the chapters that follow is worshipful response to the glory of God's mercy. That means that in this section of Scripture, Paul is not shaming us ("God loved you so much, surely you can love others"). His commands are certainly not transactional ("If you love them, God will love you"). Instead, Paul is teaching us how to rightly channel the power of God we've received as objects of his mercy. The more you understand God's mercy, the more your heart will be primed to love.[2]

---

2 None of this means that we can simply flip a switch and suddenly begin to love with divine strength. In that regard, we should keep in mind the caveat of Romans 15:14–16 with which Paul closes this section of Scripture we've just begun to explore. There, he assures the Roman Christians that he's not told them anything new (15:14) but

Mercy Changes the Heart

Let me share a story to illustrate how this works. When Sipho and his wife walked through the doors of a church in their new neighborhood, it was like being transported to a different planet. Both had grown up in Zulu-speaking Zionist churches in South Africa. But with Sipho's job transfer to Australia, they were visiting this Presbyterian church for the first time and "all our Zuluness went out the window." Back home, the clothes one wore to church were so important, Sipho's family would start preparing their church uniform on Friday afternoon. Here, with even the pastor dressed in shorts and flip-flops, things were casual to the point of feeling offensive. At home, the idea of *planning* Sunday worship would seem to be an imposition on the Holy Spirit, with services sometimes continuing all day. Here, services started promptly at 10:30 and ended at noon. At home was familiar Zulu culture. Here, Sipho and his family were alone in a sea of curious White faces. Could Zulu Zionist and Australian Presbyterian be any more distant on the ecclesiological spectrum? There was a part of Sipho that wanted to run away and never come back. Perhaps church could wait until they were safely home again.

Yet amidst all this discomfort, one thing captivated Sipho's attention that morning. It was the mercy of God. Instead of the familiar Zionist message of earning God's love through obedience, this pastor was teaching that Jesus had fulfilled the requirements of God's law *for us*. For Sipho, such mercy was revolutionary.

---

has written "by way of reminder" (15:15). So we should view Paul's teaching in these chapters not as a magic formula ("12 Steps to Genuine Love") but, as I said earlier, a set of perspectives, so that we might see difficult relationships from a different angle, in a different gospel light. Over time, these different perspectives will change us.

And this mercy kept Sipho coming back. As he continued learning of all that God had done for him in Christ, his heart warmed toward a God who had always seemed to be more stern taskmaster than affectionate father. That made him want to love God better; it made him want to love God's people better, even this congregation that was so foreign, and in whose eyes he was so foreign. Beyond that, he kept coming back because he wanted to know more of Christ's mercy. And it was in this unfamiliar church that he was seeing Christ clearly for the first time. Church was decidedly uncomfortable, to be sure. But Christ was better than comfort.

Christ Is Better Than Comfort

This realization is one that at some point we must all make about our churches: Christ is better than comfort. Some, like Sipho, must believe this just to walk through the door. Others come to this realization slowly over time. But if you are to love a church as Christ calls you to, you must believe that Christ is better than comfort. In fact, I'm hard pressed to think of a phrase that more accurately—and positively—summarizes how God's mercy enables us to embrace sacrificial love in the church. You might think of "Christ is better than comfort" as a Romans 12:1–inspired mantra to remind you how to love when love becomes difficult.

- *"Christ is better . . ."* As we discover his mercy, we will discover the surpassing worth of Christ.
- *". . . than comfort."* As we discover the surpassing worth of Christ, we will pursue him through sacrifice.

Perhaps in part because he'd tried to earn God's favor for so long, the free abundance of God's mercy was especially rich for Sipho. As a result, he loved Christ dearly. And while this church where he saw Christ was uncomfortable, Christ's mercy drew him in and compelled him toward love.

In God's kindness, Sipho's love did not go unreturned, because the people in his new church were loving him through the power of Christ's mercy as well. Outside the church, he felt like a museum curiosity, with people interrupting him to touch his hair and ask what it was like being Black. Inside this church—discomfort not withstanding—he was beginning to feel like family. People genuinely wanted his friendship. They talked honestly about their struggles to grow in Christ, "making the Bible come alive to me." It was in this church that for the first time in his life Sipho truly found Jesus. And it was in this church—this church that on the surface felt so foreign and different—that Sipho found affectionate fellowship like nothing he'd ever experienced.

I'd never suggest that the burden should be solely on a person like Sipho to adjust to an uncomfortable church. Yet what he believed was powerful: Christ *is* better than comfort. So much better. Before you became a Christian, you did what appealed to your comfort-loving nature. But once you experienced his mercy and became a Christian, you received a new nature, one that loves Christ more than comfort. That means that while some friendships at church are friendships you'd probably enjoy even if you weren't a Christian, others aren't naturally comfortable at all. But you can form warm, affectionate friendships by leaning into your new, Christ-loving nature because *he* is the one you share with these people.

The problem is that most of us aren't very good at this second kind of friendship, which is why we struggle to be in church with "those people." Of all the pitfalls I'll touch on in this book, it may be here that our consumer instincts hurt us most. If we're to travel the path I mentioned earlier, from avoiding, to tolerating, to obligatory love, to genuine friendship, we will need to be like Sipho. Like him, we must truly grasp the mercy God has shown us. And like him, we must look for Christ in our friendships at church, wagering that Christ is worth more than comfort.

A Pathway to Supernatural Joy

Do you see how this is so much more enduring and satisfying than a "white-knuckling it" kind of love, where you merely love the difficult ones in your church because you ought to love them? "Christ is better than comfort" is the pathway to real, supernatural joy in friendship because—counterintuitively—relationships at church with those whom you share little in common have potential to be your deepest, most satisfying friendships. After all, to provide an example, which is a better foundation for friendship: a shared love of football or a shared love of Christ? Build a friendship on love of football *and* love of Christ and you'll talk about Jesus, to be sure . . . and a lot about football. Build a friendship where Jesus is all you share, and what do you talk about? Jesus, of course. And Jesus is vastly superior to anything else as a foundation for friendship. This "Christ-alone" friendship will take more time to develop, and it will require more charity and patience. But it will be a gold mine of joy for you and glory to God.

To whatever extent you play it safe and invest only in friendships at church where you share much in common, you aren't putting "Christ is better than comfort" to the test. And you're depriving yourself of real joy. Especially at first, Sipho had to believe that Christ is better than comfort just to walk through the doors of his church. But consider those who fit in more naturally. They could be in a church for years, making friends with those who are easy to love, feeling included and involved, yet never realizing that a non-Christian could have a very similar experience. The thing they love about church—how wonderfully comfortable it is—threatens spiritual *danger*! Real joy in the Christian life comes when we love in ways that are only possible because of the Spirit, and comfortable love rarely does that.

Maturing Affections

Few of us are like Sipho. That's especially true of people like me, who fit in quite naturally at their churches. Our "choosing Christ over comfort" muscles are weak and underdeveloped because we're unaccustomed to channeling God's mercy into sacrificial love. Those muscles will need to be strengthened if we're to build genuine friendships where we don't see eye-to-eye on much, other than the glory of Jesus. What do we do about this? In Romans 12, Paul offers us a way forward. A spiritual weight-training class, you might say, to grow our ability to *delight* in choosing Christ over comfort. This class began in Romans 12:1, where we saw that the power of sacrificial love is found in the mercy of God. It will continue in verse 2, where we discover a key motivation for such love: the reputation of Jesus.

Questions for Reflection and Discussion

1. In what ways has God taught you about the depths of his mercy toward you?

2. How can you grow further in your appreciation of God's mercy?

3. How can the idea that Christ is better than comfort enrich your attitude toward church?

Prayer Points

- Pray that you would increasingly understand the mercy that God has shown to you.
- Pray that your congregation would act as if Christ is worth more than comfort.
- Pray that your church leaders would be skilled at showing the congregation how glorious Jesus really is.

3

What If I Don't *Want*
to Love "Them"?

Truth 3: Disunity at Church Lies about Jesus

Do not be conformed to this world, but be
transformed by the renewal of your mind, that by
testing you may discern what is the will of God,
what is good and acceptable and perfect.

ROMANS 12:2

No Backbone in the Pulpit?

Jude and Mary were having a tough time at church. Protests against various social injustices were popping up all around their city, and nearly every day they were reading enthusiastic posts from fellow church members on social media. Some posts even called on church leaders to speak up in favor of the marches,

53

which felt like veiled criticism of their pastor for not saying more. Jude and Mary felt otherwise. "They don't think he's supportive *enough*?" Jude asked incredulously. "Like he should be supportive at all! I'll tell you what that man needs. He needs some backbone. He needs to condemn this thing as the anti-Christian movement it is. Social justice is great and all, but *this* is only going to pervert justice. When is our pastor going to get the courage to tell the truth?"

Jude decided to email their pastor. It was a firm email, but kind and supportive. Mary helped him write it. And the pastor was a reasonable man. No doubt he would agree with Jude's concerns.

But to Jude's dismay, their pastor seemed entirely unconvinced by the email. He thanked Jude for engaging him. He told him he loved his and Mary's concern for truth, which is why he preached the Bible week after week. Yet he also explained his pastoral burden to protect the unity of the church and the reputation of Christ, which meant protecting the freedom of Christians to disagree on matters like these.

"Hold on," Jude emailed back, now feeling some heat. "You want to stay above the fray and just preach the Bible. But preaching means applying Scripture to what's going on around us. You can't preach the Bible *without* opposing these protests." These church members were leading people astray, after all. They were even dividing the church. Why couldn't their pastor see that?

People Who Are Hard to Love

What's tough about disagreements like this is that they touch on issues that are important yet unclear. Issues of justice are important. We can't file them into the "morally relative" folder. Yet the Bible does not always offer a clear position that all Christians must share.

Beyond that, disagreeing with other Christians on important yet unclear matters can make them hard to love. If we're honest, these people can at times feel like enemies. After all, isn't that what an enemy is? Someone whose sense of justice directly opposes your own?

Think about Simon the Zealot, who presumably wanted Palestine freed from Roman rule. In John 13, he's listening to Jesus alongside Matthew, who collected taxes for Rome. Do you wonder if these two disciples ever had trouble loving each other? Roman occupation of ancient Palestine may not seem like a big deal to us, but it was to them. What abuses had Simon and his family suffered at the hands of Roman soldiers? Or from Roman tax collectors like Matthew? And what is it he hears Jesus telling them? "By this all people will know that you are my disciples, if you have love for one another" (John 13:35). Simon casts a sideways glance at Matthew, and wonders how he's not going to lose his mind. He's supposed to love this traitor? *This* is how the Jesus he loves will be shown to the world? Seriously? How?

Perhaps you sometimes feel the same. There are people in your church you're supposed to love, but you don't want to. Maybe it's their politics. Maybe it's their personality. Sure, you can fake it. Plaster on that smile. But you don't actually love them. What's more, you don't *want* to love them.

That's certainly how Jude and Mary felt. It was increasingly difficult to tolerate what was going on in their church. Things came to a head when the pastor invited them over one evening to pick up where their email exchange had left off. As he explained that he didn't plan on speaking up for or against the protests, Jude and Mary felt angrier than ever. Finally, the pastor turned the conversation. "Jude, Mary, I love you guys. But it seems like this disagreement is making church into a really challenging place for you. You don't want to be in a church that makes you angry, and I don't want to make you angry. There are plenty of pastors in town who are saying what you wish I'd say. I'd miss you terribly if you left, but if this church is causing you to stumble, maybe you should go to one of those churches instead."

If Jude and Mary were mad before, now they were incensed. Walking to their car, Mary steamed. "How dare he tell us to go somewhere else? Like *we're* the problem? Well, maybe we *should* leave."

But the next morning, they were more circumspect. "I've been thinking more about that conversation last night, and why it made us so angry," Jude said. "I don't know about you, but the idea that we'd ever leave this church is just gut-wrenching. I mean, I really do love these people. Despite their boneheaded ideas about justice."

"Yes, despite those *boneheaded* ideas," his wife laughed. "But I think there's more," she added reflectively. "Leaving our church over something like this almost makes me embarrassed for *Jesus*. Like we both know deep down that Jesus should be enough to keep us here."

"You mean, leaving would suggest that our politics matter more than Jesus?"

"I guess so," said Mary. "Shouldn't the gospel be enough to hold this church together?"

Something Deeper: Christ's Reputation

Sometimes we need to be confronted by the possibility of losing something to realize how important it really is. That was Jude and Mary's experience. Though it would take several months to fully internalize, what they discovered that morning was the depth of their love for their church. It was a love that depended not on their shared politics but on something even deeper: Jesus Christ and his glory.

How can we learn to love people in our churches we don't want to love? By considering the glory of the one we share, and what it says about him when we act as if he's not enough to hold us together.

This is the thinking Paul calls us to in Romans 12:2: "Do not be conformed to this world, but be transformed by the renewal of your mind, that by testing you may discern what is the will of God, what is good and acceptable and perfect." Paul tells the Romans to stop thinking like the world around them—a world that would keep Jew and Gentile comfortably separated. Instead, their thinking should be transformed so they can love. The word the ESV translates as "discern" refers to the acceptance of something as genuine (thus "prove" in the NASB). Through love, the Roman Christians will prove God's will—his "crazy" will for churches made of Jews *and* Gentiles—to be what it really is, "good and acceptable and perfect." Similarly, *you* should stop thinking like the world does. Instead, love in such a way as to demonstrate the wisdom and beauty of God's plan for your church. Love to protect *his* reputation.

As was the case for Jude and Mary, the reputation of Christ often seems vague and theoretical until some situation suddenly wakes us up and we realize we're acting as if he's not as strong and as good as he really is. This is a theme Paul often goes to in his letters. Consider his teaching on marriage in Ephesians 5, where he encourages a husband to love his wife because, in doing so, he is showing off the love of Christ. Or when the church at Corinth found itself full of disagreement and disunity (like Jude and Mary's church), Paul's rebuke is strikingly theological: "Is *Christ* divided?" (1 Cor. 1:13).[1] In other words, "People, these petty fights aren't just about you. Think about what they say about *Christ*. You're his body, after all!"

Jude and Mary had tasted the love of Christ. And they knew how much Christ loved the people at church whom, at least at the moment, they couldn't stand. All this added new weight to the passage in Romans 14 that their pastor had just preached on, where Paul exhorts us to love for the sake of Christ's reputation:

> So do not let what you regard as good be spoken of as evil. For the kingdom of God is not a matter of eating and drinking but of righteousness and peace and joy in the Holy Spirit. Whoever thus serves Christ is acceptable to God and approved by men. So then let us pursue what makes for peace and for mutual upbuilding. (Rom. 14:16–19)

Some context: Romans 14 was written to Christians who disagreed over matters like which foods were permissible for Christians to eat. Here, Paul is speaking to those who rightly understood

---

1 It seems that Paul wrote Romans from Corinth, with division in Corinth in the recent past (compare Rom. 15:26 with 2 Cor. 8:1–10). Perhaps Paul wrote Romans 12–15 in part to prevent the kind of factions in Rome that he had to address in Corinth.

that Jesus had given them freedom to eat anything. But he warns them that there are larger issues at stake than being right in this argument over food. Exercise this gospel freedom (the "good") without regard for love, and it will be mocked as evil. That's what is at stake when we judge and despise those we disagree with. If our churches are mainly known for judging one another, Paul says, not only will they not be acceptable to God but even people will despise them. And rightly so.

Making Church Unity Paramount

Paul's charge to love the reputation of Christ should put our dis-agreements over Christian-freedom issues into perspective. This doesn't suggest, of course, that *all* disagreements in a church are Christian-freedom issues. Recall from the first chapter of this book that the differences I have in mind aren't those that jeopardize the gospel. If, for instance, the protests in Jude and Mary's city were promoting physician-assisted suicide, then the pastor *would* be wrong to act as if Christians can stand on both sides of the issue. The situations where we can learn from Jude and Mary's experi-ence are those where we *should* be able to maintain unity in Christ despite differences in background or conviction.

In that regard, we should note that Paul isn't encouraging Chris-tians to become "squishy," unwilling to stand on their convictions for fear of offending others. Quite the contrary. In Romans 14 (which we'll discuss more in a few chapters), he is extremely protective of Christian conviction, even when convictions in the church collide. Rather, Paul is telling us that very often, there's more at stake than conviction alone. When the reputation of Christ in his church looms large, a deeper and more extensive set of concerns shapes our values, increasing our wisdom as we seek to speak the truth in love.

For example, suppose you feel as if the biggest issue facing your church is a raging debate about whether young mothers should work outside the home. In fact, the bigger issue is whether you can work through that disagreement in a way that honors Christ. You can win the battle but lose the war.

The kingdom of God, Paul says in Romans 14:17, is a matter of "righteousness and peace and joy in the Holy Spirit." I love the crescendo of that triad. Your church should be known not merely for being right but for *righteousness*—for doing what is right in all things, including in your love. Your church should also be known for *peace*. Peace with God creates peace between his children. And your church should be known for its *joy*. Not a gritted-teeth "putting up" with one another (though obedience sometimes needs to start there). But the joy of the bride, enraptured with the bridegroom. Righteousness, peace, and joy. What a wonderful prayer list for your church!

Unity is especially critical when a church encounters waves of opposition from the world outside. Imagine that your local government outlaws parents evangelizing their own children. Some parents in your church want to quietly disobey the law, teaching their children about Jesus carefully and in secret. Others call such an approach cowardly and instead "courageously" set up an outdoor Sunday school, daring the authorities to act. The "careful" in the church, meanwhile, fear that the "courageous" are foolishly making a bad situation worse. One of these approaches may eventually prove to be best. But what both groups of Christians must remember is that the greatest threat to the gospel is not this new law, but its ability to divide the church into warring camps. There are exceptions, of course, when unity is no longer our primary concern. But in general, when your church encounters disagreements, unity should be your paramount concern. After all, what did Jesus repeatedly pray for in John 17, knowing his followers would be hated by the world (17:14)? "That they may all be one, just as you, Father, are in me, and I in you" (17:21). So often, the path to apostasy during persecution is not the direct incentive that persecution creates to deny the faith, but a fracturing of church unity under pressure, which itself leads to a slow erosion of faith.

How to Grow in Cherishing Christ's Reputation

Impressed anew with the power of Christ-centered unity to proclaim the worth of Christ, Jude and Mary began a very different chapter in their life at church. They didn't leave. And as time went on, their pastor was glad they hadn't. None of their concerns about this "justice" movement of the day changed, but their posture toward the members they disagreed with began to change. Their sense of urgency over the larger political issues didn't change, but the unity of the church began to feel more urgent. Societal concerns moved a few steps into the background, and concern for church unity shifted into the foreground. Sometimes they had to bite their tongues. When they did discuss political issues, they worked hard to keep their cool. Sometimes they'd rehearse to themselves biblical truths like those we've discussed in this chapter. Yet increasingly, with transformed hearts and renewed minds set on God's "good and acceptable and pleasing" will (Rom. 12:2), they became bridge-builders to those on the other side of these issues. While some in the church began to agree with Jude and Mary, many did not, but Jude and Mary didn't love them any less fervently.

Jude and Mary discovered a new desire to love their church by seeing how Christ had staked some of his reputation on the unity of their church. But too often we love our *own* reputations above his. How can we grow in this area?

First, we must learn to see our own self-righteousness. This has been my own experience. There was a time in my Christian life when the words "I love Jesus" honestly felt more academic than adoring. To be sure, I loved Jesus for what he had done for me. But I didn't appreciate him as beautiful, glorious, and delightful, at least not as I do today. I loved the idea of Jesus more than the person. Yet a new layer of love for him emerged as I began to grasp my own self-righteousness. Discovering that I was quite difficult, and yet Christ had shown me patience, I began to marvel at his forbearance. Discovering that the things I wanted for my life were dull and empty but what he wanted for me was delightful and satisfying, I began to marvel at his goodness. Discovering the evil of my heart, I began to marvel at his mercy and grace. Discovering the beauty and perfection of Scripture, I began to marvel at his beauty and perfection. Just as falling in love with my wife made me zealous for her reputation, so falling in love with Jesus Christ grew a zeal for his glory to be known and delighted in.

Second, we must take the time to stare at Christ—like those in John 12:21, who came saying, "We wish to see Jesus." "All Scripture is breathed out by God" (2 Tim. 3:16), and yet the Gospels should claim a special place for all who want hearts captivated by Christ. If you feel like the phrase "for the glory of Christ" is hollow and unmotivating, study through Matthew or Mark or

Luke or John and learn to marvel at Jesus. Books like *Seeing and Savoring Jesus Christ* by John Piper or *The Bruised Reed* by Richard Sibbes can be good aids in this endeavor. Do you need motivation to study theology? Investigating the perfections of the Godhead is a booster shot for our affections.

Third, recognize that a desire for Christ's reputation can start in one area of life and spread to others. We bear the reputation of Christ in many ways because, ultimately, he is Lord over all of life. As parents, we reflect our heavenly Father to our kids (Eph. 3:14–15). As laborers, we work ultimately for Jesus (Col. 3:23). We do that in marriage (Eph. 5:22–33), and of course, at church. You might begin to cherish the reputation of Christ in one arena of life before the rest. For me, it started when I got married and was staggered by the truth that my actions communicated to my wife what Christ is like, for good or for ill. As Christ's reputation became a controlling influence in that part of my life, it spread to the workplace, then my parenting, and finally to my love at church.

Finding a Deeper Love

What exactly happened inside Jude and Mary? How did anger at their pastor's words eventually lead to love? What happened is that when pushed, they discovered a love of Christ's reputation in their church that was stronger than their aversions. It was a love for the glory of Christ that was higher, deeper, wider, and longer than any other concern in this world. How does that happen for the rest of us? We can't simply decide to have such a love. After all, the love of Jesus's followers is to be a love with divine strength. "This is my commandment, that you love one another *as I have loved you*" (John 15:12). The secret to loving *each other* as he has loved us is loving *him* for how he has loved us—and not wanting anything to detract from the glory of his love.

A love for Christ's reputation in your church fosters love for your church. Yet aren't there a few people in your church who make this especially difficult? Wouldn't the whole endeavor work better if some of them would simply go to a different church? That leads to the next truth we must consider: you belong together.

Questions for Reflection and Discussion

1. What has helped you to grow in cherishing the reputation of Christ?

2. Can you think of an example in your life when a desire to protect Jesus's reputation led you to change what you were doing or considering doing?

3. What can you do to help your church rightly prioritize the value of unity in conflict or disagreement?

Prayer Points

- Pray that the reputation of Christ would become more of a controlling influence in your life.
- Pray that your congregation would be known for righteousness, peace, and joy.
- Pray that your church leaders would be jealous for the reputation of Christ in your church.

4

Wouldn't We Be Better Off without "Them"?

Truth 4: You Belong Together

For as in one body we have many members, and
the members do not all have the same function,
so we, though many, are one body in Christ,
and individually members one of another.

ROMANS 12:4–5

People You'd Rather Avoid

"Wouldn't we be better off without some of these people?"

Do you ever wonder that? Even as a pastor, I'm afraid sometimes I do. I know Paul wrote that "the parts of the body that seem to be weaker are indispensable" (1 Cor. 12:22). But couldn't some of them be indispensable to someone *else's* church body?

Your church is to be a family, the household of God (Eph. 2:19), yet the temptation is strong to give up being the kind of family we dream of. Instead, we settle for the kind of family too many of us grew up in, where we looked out for ourselves and family mealtimes were a tenuous truce, with TV as a peace-keeping distraction. Very often, our attitude toward the "unlovables" in church could be summarized as "I don't need them, and I don't owe them anything. So can't I just avoid them?"

If the purpose of church were purely utilitarian, settling for such coexistence wouldn't be that bad. In fact, people would probably be *happier* if they could avoid those at church who rub them the wrong way. And if people are happier, they'll likely serve more and give more, which will enable the church to accomplish more.

But remember, the purpose of a church goes beyond the merely utilitarian; it is to be a beautiful reflection of the glory of Christ. In fact, mere coexistence is the gateway to factions. If the Acts 6 Christians I mentioned earlier had settled for coexistence, with separate deacon teams for each faction, wouldn't that have simply played into Satan's narrative? "Nothing to see here, folks. Nothing remarkable about the Christians." Isn't that the story Satan wants the world to believe about *your* church?

Catherine, a woman in my church, was having this exact struggle. When a man named Jason first joined her church, she cringed. She despised his vocal opinions on a multitude of issues. She thought his ideas were a menace to society and was embarrassed that a fellow *Christian* would be known for them. So when he moved away and joined another church, she breathed a sigh of relief.

But a few years later, she caught sight of him again—now happily married (yay!), living just a few minutes away (yikes!), and once again a member of her church (oh no!). At first, she tried the strategy of benign toleration. Yet she found that unsettling. On the one hand, there was nothing wrong with her and Jason never interacting. After all, they'd never been close and the congregation was large. Yet surely it wasn't right to loathe someone she called "brother," even if they never talked.

This is, in fact, the challenge Paul addresses in Romans 12:3–8. "Wouldn't we be better off without some of these people?" These verses walk us through two movements our hearts must make if, like Catherine, we want a satisfying answer to this burning question. First, we must understand that in Christ we *need* each other (even people like Jason). And second, that people like Catherine and Jason *belong* together. Let's take each in turn.

We Need Each Other

To understand the context behind these verses in Romans 12, we must look back to Romans 11. There, Paul addresses Gentiles who think that ethnic Israel is forever excluded from God's family because they've rejected Jesus. Twice Paul warns Gentiles not to arrogantly despise Israel (Rom. 11:20, 25) because God loves them (11:28).

Then in Romans 12, with the Jew-Gentile churches of Rome in view, Paul continues this message of humility.

For by the grace given to me I say to everyone among you not to think of himself more highly than he ought to think, but to think with sober judgment, each according to the measure of faith that God has assigned. For as in one body we have many members, and the members do not all have the same function, so we, though many, are one body in Christ. (12:3–5)

In other words, the idea that you'd be better off without "them" is fueled by pride (12:3). The Gentile Christians *needed* their Jewish brothers and sisters in Christ, just as a body needs all its members. In this, Thomas Watson's advice is apt: "A humble Christian studies his own infirmities, and another's excellencies."[1]

The good news, Paul tells us, is that reality is the enemy of pride. As we "think with sober judgment," seeing the truth about ourselves and others, pride will diminish. Perhaps even your flesh's insistence that you'd be better off without "those people" can foster humility, as you confess such pride as sin and bring your assessment of yourself a step closer to the truth.

The reality that you'll see, as you wipe the fog of pride from your eyes, is that you and your church are in fact incomplete without "those" people, which is the point of Paul's image of the church as a body in Romans 12:5. As he writes elsewhere, its members are different by design. "The eye cannot say to the hand, 'I have no need of you,' nor again the head to the feet, 'I have no need of you.' On the contrary, the parts of the body that seem to be weaker are indispensable, and on those parts of the body that we think less honorable we bestow the greater honor" (1 Cor. 12:21–23).

Do you really believe that? If you've been a Christian for long, this image of the church as a body is no doubt familiar. But have

---

1 Thomas Watson, *The Godly Man's Picture Drawn with a Scripture-Pencil, or, Some Characteristic Marks of a Man Who Is Going to Heaven* (1666; Carlisle, PA: Banner of Truth, 2003), 79.

you thought of it in terms of the people in your church whom you dislike, disagree with, and are tempted to despise? You *need* them. Why?

You Need Their Faith

Personally, I can see my need for others in my church most clearly when I think in terms of faith. Not "I need their skills" or "I need their wisdom" or "I need their perspective" (though all of this may be true) but "I need their faith."

In particular, you need their faith to encourage you. Consider a man named Joseph as an example. A Christian since his early twenties, his identity was firmly in Christ. Yet living in Nairobi, far from his ancestral roots in the West of Kenya, his tribal identity as a Luo was also important. Joseph and his wife had one child, Paul—their pride and joy—whom they'd raised to appreciate his Luo heritage and to treasure the truths of the gospel. Given where they lived, they'd always gone to a church that was majority Kikuyu, a tribe whose position of power was insufferable to many Luo. In fact, it was just last year that Joseph's two-year-old niece had been killed in a spate of anti-Luo violence, instigated by a Kikuyu politician.

Imagine, then, the constellation of emotions in Joseph's heart the day Paul came home from university with Marie on his arm, a godly, delightful, *Kikuyu* young woman whom Paul hoped to marry. Now imagine the thoughts of that majority Kikuyu congregation on Paul and Marie's wedding day. For them, the idea of marrying one's only son off to a Kikuyu family wouldn't cause so much as a stir. But for Joseph? For him, this was a challenge of faith. Did he really believe that Christ was worth more than tribe? As such, Joseph's radiant smile on Paul and Marie's wedding day was a special encouragement to this congregation because they saw in him a special example of faith. His faith was encouraging precisely because of their tribal differences, and it demonstrated with power that Christ was worth more.

When someone without much formal education joins my rather educated congregation, I'm encouraged by his faith. When I see someone at church embraced by a friend group who disagrees with her politics, I'm encouraged by their faith. The faith of those in your church with whom you differ is especially encouraging because they're taking risks for Jesus in places you might not have to.

That's one reason you need the faith of those who differ. Here's another: you need their faith because it protects your faith. As Proverbs 27:17 says, "Iron sharpens iron, / and one man sharpens another." There's nothing inherently wrong with being in a church where everyone agrees on a wide variety of nonessential issues.[2] Yet such uniformity can be dangerous because statements that are rhetorically powerful yet biblically sloppy are not challenged. It's dangerous because, for example, our shared politics, rather than Scripture, can slip into the driver's seat of our convictions, and this can lead to unbiblical compromise. It's those who share our faith yet disagree with us on nonessential matters who are often best positioned to protect us from error.

Trying to Understand

Catherine had read Romans 12. She'd read 1 Corinthians 12. She *knew* that Jason was indispensable. But how? That was a question

---

2 By "nonessential issues" I mean issues one can disagree on and still be members of the same church—which is often a higher bar than merely "essential for salvation." We'll explore this more in the final chapters of this book.

she couldn't answer. So she asked for help. She called Shawn, who shared her disagreements with Jason—but who had been Jason's close friend for years.

"Shawn, I need your help. I'm having a hard time now that Jason's back. To be honest, I despise the man. I know that's terrible and sinful, but it's true, and I just can't seem to shake what I feel. I know you disagree with him too. It would help me if you could explain the good you see in him."

For the next few minutes, Shawn patiently shared with her about Jason's unsurpassed loyalty as a friend. "You and I both know I'm never going to ask his advice on social issues. But if I were ever in trouble, he'd be the first person I'd call. I know he'd do anything to help me out of a tough spot. And the very fact that we disagree on so much is what makes his loyalty to me so meaningful."

I admire Catherine for wanting that conversation. It was precisely the opposite of what we so often do when placed in her shoes, venting frustration about those we dislike through gossip and slander. And for Catherine, the conversation with Shawn was helpful. Now whenever she saw Jason, she thought of the role he played in Shawn's life, which began to warm her heart toward Jason. It wasn't so much that she'd discovered a need *she* had for Jason—but she was starting to see how he was needed.

Loving merely because we ought to love can be a "better than them" kind of love, where we stoop down to lift up our benighted inferiors. But whereas obligation so quickly fuels pride, need is the language of humility. As such, a belief that we really do in fact *need* one another is a critical step toward genuine fellowship in the local church.

We Belong to Each Other

Catherine's story wasn't finished though. What Shawn said certainly helped quiet the unholy thoughts that threatened to invade her mind when she saw Jason in the hallway after the service. But something about it felt disturbingly utilitarian. "Should I love him merely because he meets a need in our church? What if I'd never discovered that need?" After all, who was *she* to presume that she could discover God's purposes for every member of her church? "And besides," she mused, "I'm supposed to love Jason as Christ has loved me (John 15:12). Jesus doesn't love me simply because I meet a need. So why should that be the reason I love Jason?"

Fortunately, these verses in Romans 12 contain yet more wisdom. While "we need each other" is a better foundation for friendship than "I ought to love them," it's insufficient. Such a perspective can still feed a consumerist, what's-in-it-for-me mentality. As those who have soaked our whole lives in the waters of modern consumerism, the rest of Paul's teaching in these verses is critical. Specifically, he moves on from "we need each other" to "we belong to each other." Which is profound.

Members One of Another

We see this shift in verses 4 and 5, where Paul discusses his image of the church as a body. "For as in one body we have many members, and the members do not all have the same function, so we, though many, are one body in Christ." We're not only sinners made alive; we're strangers made one. As such, I would have expected this verse to conclude by noting that we are "individually members of *his* body," emphasizing that we belong to *Christ*.

Instead, Paul writes "and individually members *one of another*."[3] Because we belong to Christ, we belong to one another.

Just roll that last phrase around in your mind for a moment. "Individually members one of another." For the Christian, identity is fundamentally corporate; we belong to one another. Why is that? Because we began new life through the same Savior, and through the same Savior we have the same future. Or, as Charles Spurgeon put it, "Every saint is shot from the same bow, and is speeding towards the same target."[4] Accordingly, Paul's emphasis in the next verses is not our need *for* one another but our service *to* one another, service we provide with abundance, cheerfulness, and zeal (12:8). Abundance, cheer, and zeal are evidence of *delighted* obligation, not of heartless obligation. So how does this idea that "we belong to one another" result in delight?

The answer is in how such "belonging" shapes how we experience an obligation to love. Consider a blended family that forms when mom and dad marry after being widowed or divorced (which echoes Paul's agricultural "ingrafting" analogy that precedes this passage, in Rom. 11). The feeling of belonging that produces abundance, cheer, and zeal isn't what the siblings feel on day one, when "you belong to them" means "you *ought* to love them." It's more like what you feel in year ten, if things go well, where you *want* to love because you belong together as a family. Paul teaches something similar in 1 Corinthians 7 when he tells

---

3   Paul does the same in 1 Corinthians 12, where he begins by talking about our need for one another (12:21) and transitions to the truth that we belong to one another (12:27).

4   Charles Spurgeon, "Unity in Christ," vol. 12, *Metropolitan Tabernacle Pulpit*, preached January 7, 1866, the Spurgeon Center, www.spurgeon.org.

a husband and wife that they belong to one another (1 Cor. 7:4), which leads not to selfish taking, but selfless giving (7:3). That is, not ground for abuse ("you belong to me") but a beautiful, self-forgetful love ("I belong to you"). Such love sees it as only natural and fitting to give itself in service to the other.[5]

Just as your praise belongs to God, and all is not right until you give it to him, your love belongs to your brothers and sisters at church, and all is not right until you give it to them. In that sense, Paul's words here shouldn't function as a command ("act as if you belong together") but as an invitation ("discover that you really do belong together").

They Are Worthy of Your Love

This was, in fact, the next stage of Catherine's journey. A week later, she was back on the phone with Shawn, explaining her latest dilemma. Shawn seemed to get it right away. "Right. Trying to feel brotherly affection for Jason simply because he meets a need feels like a friendship built on performance, not grace." Catherine hadn't thought about it this way, but it certainly made

---

5   Consider all the parallels between the church and marriage. Both have a task to accomplish: the church's is the Great Commission (Matt. 28:19–20); marriage's is fruitfulness (Gen. 1:28). The power to accomplish the task lies in the participants' differences: the church needs all of its members (1 Cor. 12), and husband and wife were designed to complement each other (Gen. 2:18). The value of neither (the church or marriage) can be pigeonholed into the accomplishment of its task. Instead, the value of both is reflective (Eph. 3:10 for the church, Eph. 5:22–33 for marriage). As a result, we see mutual belonging in both church and marriage. We are "individually members one of another" in Romans 12; in marriage, a husband's body belongs to his wife and vice versa (1 Cor. 7:4). Consider how brittle and heartless marriage becomes when it is merely about accomplishing the task or about mutual fulfillment of need. Instead, the joy of marriage is in the beauty of self-giving love. And so it is for the church.

sense. "Catherine, the need Jason meets in my life isn't the whole answer to your question of how to love him. It's an invitation to discover something deeper." The reason Jason was so loyal, Shawn explained, wasn't because he was naturally a loyal person, but because of the transformation the Holy Spirit had worked in his heart. And the Spirit's work is never an end in itself; it always points to Christ (John 16:14–15). "Christ's handiwork is all over that man, even if he's still a work in progress, and that can help you see Christ in him. Christ is in you, Christ is in Jason, and that means you belong together. You're both adopted by God, and so you're family. Because of Christ, Jason is *worthy* of your love."

That word resonated with Catherine, and I hope it resonates with you also. The other members of your church are *worthy* of your love because in Christ you belong together. If you treat them as undeserving of your time and energy and concern, Jesus Christ himself stands up to object. They are *worthy* to receive your abundant, cheerful, and zealous service because in Christ you belong to them. With that, the locus of love's power has moved from you and your obligations, or you and your needs, to Christ, because in Christ you belong to them. That's how we shift from loving merely because we must, to loving with delight.[6]

Indeed, the very fact that this worthiness is grounded in Christ and not in ourselves makes for a special kind of joy in friendship. Here's an analogy: I once had the privilege of giving away a house

---

6 I've learned about this "belonging to them" kind of love by watching some in my church whom the world lauds as important, such as military generals or business leaders. Perhaps because they've attained so much in the world's eyes, they delight to lavish patient love on the weak and struggling in my church. And they tell me of a special delight that comes from using worldly stature to showcase the Christ-given worthiness of even the "least" of God's children.

to a family in my church. The house wasn't mine, and it wasn't for keeps—but it was free for two years. And it wasn't just any house; it was a fabulous, architectural masterpiece. The owner asked if I knew of a good use for it, I mentioned this family, and he agreed. "You'll enjoy telling them the good news," I said to the owner. But he replied, "The house belongs to the Lord. You tell them yourself."

I called the husband of this family and asked him to meet me nearby. As we walked toward the house, he told me how discouraged he and his wife were because they had no permanent place to live. I unlocked the door and we went inside. "Whose place is this?" he asked, "and why do you have a key?" "It's yours," I told him with a smile, as I handed him the keys. For a moment he thought it was a bad joke (not uncharacteristic for me), but when I kept on smiling, he started to cry (quite uncharacteristic for him) and grabbed a chair to steady himself. "Oh my! I've got to call my wife and tell her!"

This man didn't deserve the house, and I didn't deserve to be giving it to him. And that's why this is such a special memory for both of us. The owner is the one who made me worthy to give it; the owner made this family worthy to receive it. In similar fashion, Jesus is the one who made you worthy to love his dear children, and he's the one who made them worthy of your love.

There may be many good reasons why you won't have close friendship with some members of your church. After all, unless you're in a very small church, you can't be friends with everyone. But that will never be because they are not worthy of your love.

So think about those people in your church with the noxious opinions or the grating personalities. Do they in and of themselves deserve your time, attention, hospitality, and friendship? Of course not. But because Christ gave himself for them, you belong to them, and so in giving of yourself to them there's a special kind of joy. As you seek to love—not just because you should, and not just because of what you need, but because in Christ you belong together—there is a sweetness in friendship that's unmatched in the world outside. What a testimony to the power of Christ's blood!

The Path to Genuine Love

Let's take a moment then to review Paul's argument so far in Romans 12. We see the power behind our love in verses 1–2. In verses 3–8 we see the humble posture behind Christian love. Not merely love from obligation. Not merely love from need. But love because in Christ we belong to one another. This is the path to genuine, Christ-exalting fellowship with "those" people in your church.

Let's move on to verses 9–16, where Paul continues to walk us down this path.

Questions for Discussion and Reflection

1. What are some examples of how the faith of those who differ from you (in background, opinions, convictions, etc.) has been an important encouragement for your faith?

2. How has Christ made the other members of your church to be worthy of your love?

3. Imagine that you're having a hard time getting along with a fellow church member. How does the truth that you are "members one of another" (Rom. 12:5) help?

Prayer Points

- Pray that you would more thoroughly believe that, because of Christ, even the "difficult" ones in your church are worthy of your love.
- Pray that your congregation would increasingly discover that, in God's providence, they do in fact belong together.
- Pray that your church leaders would trust God's purposes for including each and every member as part of your church body.

5

How Can I Be *Friends* with "Those" People?

Truth 5: Hope in God Creates Affection for Others

Let love be genuine. Abhor what is evil; hold fast to
what is good. Love one another with brotherly affection.
Outdo one another in showing honor. Do not be slothful
in zeal, be fervent in spirit, serve the Lord. Rejoice in
hope, be patient in tribulation, be constant in prayer.

ROMANS 12:9–12

Paul's Crazy Command

Sometimes God's commands seem absurd. This one to Moses comes to mind: "Speak to the rock" (Num. 20:8 NASB). Or Jesus's to a corpse: "Lazarus, come out" (John 11:43). Paul's command

79

in Romans 12 is right up there: "Love one another with brotherly affection" (12:10). It's easy to gloss over such good, pious language. But think for a moment. A *command* to love with *affection*?[1] How can God command the heart?

Of course, it's not just Paul who does this. Jesus told us to love God with all our *hearts* (Mark 12:30). Peter tells us to "love one another earnestly *from a pure heart*" (1 Pet. 1:22). As Bible scholar D. A. Carson writes of Jesus's command to love in Mark 12:30, "It is inadequate to think that the verb 'to love' means something narrowly volitional . . . as if Christian love can be reduced to committed altruism. The command to love must not be stripped of affective content."[2] To love with affection isn't the same as having *feelings* of love, but it's much more than a steely determination to love. To borrow Augustine's terminology, it is the will in harmony with desire.[3]

What a standard for our love! It's one thing to love those difficult people in my church and to understand that they're *worthy* of my love, as we saw in the last chapter. But now you're saying I must love *with affection*? How can I do that? Aside from just

---

1   It should be noted that while the ESV translates this phrase as "brotherly affection," many other translations use a word other than *affection*. For example, the CSB opts for "deeply as brothers and sisters" and in the NASB it's, "Be devoted to one another in brotherly love." A literal translation would be "in regard to brotherly love, with devotion." Yet whether one translates with the word *affection* or not, the bar is quite high. What Paul has in mind in your church is the kind of heartfelt love normally reserved for close family.

2   D. A. Carson, *Love in Hard Places* (Wheaton, IL: Crossway, 2002), 21.

3   Augustine, *Confessions*, 10.23.33. Categories like passions, sentiments, and affections can be more useful and precise in considering what Paul is commanding here in Romans 12 than the more modern concepts of emotions or feelings. "Affections" as inclinations of the will should be distinguished from "passions" that overtake us apart from the will.

snipping Romans 12 and 1 Peter 1 and a few other passages out of my Bible, there's no exit ramp in sight on this highway of impossibility.

Jesus's Crazy Church

Yet isn't this Jesus's design for the church? If it were within *our* power to obey this command, what would that say about *God's* power? Consider the Pharisees. They reduced the commands of Scripture to a set of rules that, with great difficulty, could be obeyed regardless of their hearts' condition. And so Jesus quotes Isaiah against them: "This people honors me with their lips, / but their heart is far from me; / in vain do they worship me" (Matt. 15:8–9). Half-hearted love through gritted teeth can flow from faith and as such it can honor God. Yet love that's full of heart, affection, and warmth is an even more perfect reflection of God's love toward us. Without denigrating the "gritted teeth" love that's often where we begin, we should aspire toward affectionate love in the church. That's in part how we make the beautiful reflection that is the church to be . . . *beautiful.*

Great Stories . . . but What about You?

Given God's heartfelt love toward us, it's no surprise that stories abound of former enemies becoming affectionate brothers and sisters in Christ. Just type something like "former enemies become one in Christ" into your internet search engine. You'll get results like Martin Seliane, an activist during South African apartheid, and Adriaan Vlok, a national security officer who sought to imprison such activists. Each learned that the other had become a Christian and "these two men who formerly longed to

see each other killed, began a friendship and ministry partner-
ship together." Referring to how the gospel destroys the wall of
hostility between believers (Eph. 2:14), Martin said, "Those are
the words in a book. This [pointing to Adriaan and himself] is
what it looks like!"[4]

These stories are not hard to find, but my real interest is you.
Are stories like Martin and Adriaan's always "out there" yet rarely
in your own church or in your own heart? Can you imagine loving the difficult ones in your church *with affection*? Or does that
fall into the "hypothetically possible but never gonna happen"
category? (Like the "God can raise the dead" category once was
for Mary and Martha.) If your ambition for love doesn't include
affection, then your ambition is too weak. So let's listen as Paul describes the kind of love we should aspire to and how we get there.

What Makes for Genuine Love

At first, the ordering of the sentences in Romans 12:9–16 appears haphazard. Yet there are some important implicit, thematic
connections between these commands (though explicit links are
admittedly lacking). As such, it is helpful to consider these verses
within a framework that connects the dots between Paul's many
admonitions.

Paul's main command is to "let love be genuine." Or in some
translations, "Let love be without hypocrisy."[5] This admonition

---

4 "Former Enemies Now Fellow Evangelists," The Master's Academy International (blog),
   April 20, 2018, https://www.tmai.org/.

5 In the original, this command does not actually have a verb but functions more as a
   heading for what follows. Literally, "genuine love." What follows then is a series of
   "participial clauses to explain just what sincere love really is," followed by a series of
   referential commands through verse 12 ("with reference to brotherly love," "with refer-

is followed by a set of commands that flesh out the *standard* for such love: it should be marked by affection, honor, and zeal (12:10–11). Next, in verse 12, Paul introduces a triad of commands that explains the *mindset* behind genuine love. Rejoice in hope, be patient in tribulation, be constant in prayer. Finally, the remaining commands explain the *outworking* of such genuine love. Give yourself to your brothers and sisters with your money and your home (12:13), your rights (12:14), your heart (12:15), and your reputation (12:16). As we'll see in a bit, the dynamo that powers everything else in this passage is that little word *hope* at the beginning of verse 12. Namely, hope that God will use your life together as a church to paint a perfect portrait of his glory.

Let's walk through these verses to see Paul's recipe for genuine love.

Paul's Standard for Genuine Love

We'll start with Paul's principal command, that love be genuine and without hypocrisy. What would make love to be hypocritical? Sometimes, the actions we call love are honestly more motivated by gain than love. Of course, there's nothing wrong with seeking help from those we know at church. But if "love for gain" is the full extent of your motivations for love, you will struggle to love where love matters most.

A second type of hypocritical love is a Pharisaical "love for show." While "love for gain" corrupts love for those who help you, "love for show" corrupts love for those who are helped *by* you. You

---

ence to honor," and so forth). See Douglas Moo, *The Epistle to the Romans*, The New International Commentary on the New Testament (Grand Rapids, MI: Eerdmans: 1996), 774, 777.

might *act* as if you love a certain person in your church, but you know your heart's not in it. God knows your heart's not in it. And let's be honest, that person probably knows it too. The tokenism I described a few chapters ago is a good example. Love for show is a common result of obedience through sheer moral fortitude. "Sure, I'll love everyone in my church . . . just watch me!" Yet God does not merely command love with action; he commands love with heart.

The trio of commands in Romans 12:10–11 further fleshes out the love Paul expects of believers: "Love one another with brotherly affection. Outdo one another in showing honor. Do not be slothful in zeal, be fervent in spirit, serve the Lord."

Genuine love is affectionate, Paul says. It shows honor. And it does this with a supernatural zeal that's fervent in spirit.[6] After all, love within the church is a primary demonstration of our love for God. It's how we "serve the Lord" (12:11). If your love has no heart, then your service to God has no heart. That's an arresting thought, isn't it? In a moment we'll see how love can be heartfelt. But first, consider all the incomplete imitations that pass for love in the church.

- "I'll love him, but you can't expect me to enjoy doing it." This "love" denies the importance of affection. Better to say, "I'll love him, and pray that affection will follow."
- "I feel sorry for her, so I'm going to go over and help her." This attitude can reduce someone to a charity case. Even

6   Scholars disagree over whether Paul's phrase "fervent in spirit" refers to *our* spirits or the *Holy* Spirit, since the two uses of the word would be identical in the original. That's why some English translations capitalize *Spirit* (e.g., CSB) and some don't (e.g., ESV). Quite possibly, Paul is using this ambiguity intentionally, challenging us with a play on the word *spirit*. True fervor in your spirit can only come from the Holy Spirit. Thus, I've described this as a *supernatural* zeal.

when helping those who are weak, our ambition should be to honor them.

- "I've invested enough in that relationship, and it's not getting any easier; I think I'm done." This is not loving with Spirit-empowered zeal.
- "I'll build a friendship with her, because I don't know many people who are [insert demographic category here]." Again, this may be a good starting point, but love that stops here could hardly be called genuine.

We must beware of complacent satisfaction with these "starter" motivations. As such, these three words—*affection*, *honor*, and *zeal*—are good to keep in mind as you evaluate the genuineness of your friendships at church. Is your friendship moving toward *affection*, or is it settled in obligation? Does your friendship *honor* the individual or debase him as a charity case? Is your desire for this person's good *zealous*, or is it half-hearted?

Of course, our still-sinful hearts will inevitably fall short in many ways. That's where we need the mindset that Paul describes next.

The Mindset behind Genuine Love

"Rejoice in hope, be patient in tribulation, be constant in prayer" (Rom. 12:12). As we'll see in a moment, there's a lot going on in this sentence, so let's look at each of these short phrases in turn.

"Rejoice in Hope"

What's striking about this phrase is its similarity to Paul's longer section on joyful hope and patient suffering in Romans 5: "Through him we have also obtained access by faith into this grace in which we stand, and we *rejoice in hope* of the glory of God" (5:2).[7] The joy of Romans 5:2 looks *back* to the undeserved riches of being justified by faith. It looks *ahead*—with hope—to "the glory of God," when the portrait God has painted of his glory in our lives will be unfurled for all to see. This hope in the glory of God is a hope that will not disappoint, Paul writes in Romans 5:5, because "God's love has been poured into our hearts through the Holy Spirit." God *will* be shown to be gracious and glorious through our lives because his love will inevitably bear fruit as it's animated by his Spirit.

It's this joyful hope of Romans 5 that Paul inserts into our quest for genuine love in Romans 12. But whereas the context of Romans 5 is your salvation as an individual, the context of Romans 12 is love together as a church. As such, in Romans 12 Paul is telling you to not merely rejoice that God will be glorified in *your* life; rejoice in the hope that God will be glorified in *their* lives, the lives of your brothers and sisters at church. Putting Romans 5 and 12 together gives us something like, "Rejoice in the hope that God is showing off his glory through our life together."

HOPE BUILDS AFFECTION

This hope is what generates the affection Paul has just written about in Romans 12:10 ("love one another with brotherly affection"). Consider as an example Paul's own affection that he describes in

---

7   The reason we should read Romans 12 in light of Romans 5 is not so much lexical as it is thematic. That is, the word translated "rejoice" in Romans 12:12 isn't the same in the original as the word translated "rejoice" in Romans 5:2 (though the two are highly related, and it's entirely appropriate to translate both with the word "rejoice," as the ESV does). However, the passages are linked by themes of joyful hope, followed by patient suffering.

Philippians 1:8, when he writes, "I yearn for you all with the affection of Christ Jesus." How do we experience the same affection for our fellow church members that Jesus has? By seeing in them what Jesus sees; that is, a reflection of *his* glory that is increasing in beauty as they become like him.[8] Learn to rejoice that the greatest good imaginable is taking place in the lives of others in your church, that through their lives Jesus's glory is being unveiled.

From beginning to end, the history of our fallen world has maligned the character of our good and merciful God. It has said his promises of justice are impotent, his assertion of sovereignty is a lie, his claims to be good are unfounded, and his authority cannot be trusted. Every sin ever committed adds to this mountain of falsehoods about the one who is perfect, delightful, and beautiful. Yet through your faith and the faith of the others in your church—including the ones you struggle to love—God is dismantling this web of slander so that we can see him for the glory of who he really is. Learn to love the glimpses you see in your church of Jesus's glory, trusting that there's more you cannot yet see, and you will learn to love your brothers and sisters with the affection of Christ.

This means that in the church we find joy—and affection—in what doesn't yet exist. We find it in the *hope* of what God is doing.[9] I see a shadow of this in the affection I feel for my children. Let's say that one of my kids goes above and beyond to do

8 Similarly, in John 15:9–12 Jesus says that as we obey his command to love each other as a reflection of his love for us (which in turn reflects his Father's love for him), the joy he has in us will become our own.

9 This is what powered the love of the Colossian church: "The love that you have for all the saints, *because* of the hope laid up for you in heaven" (Col. 1:4–5).

something kind and thoughtful for a sibling. The affection I feel in that act of love isn't a naïve belief that, from now on, my child will only ever be kind and thoughtful. Far from it! Yet there's a real joy in that hopeful glimpse of the godly man or woman I pray my child is becoming. In the same way, there's real joy when we see the glory of God beginning to shine in those around us at church, even if it's embryonic. That's a joy powered by hope.

One significant impediment to genuine affection for others in your church is the ugliness you see in their hearts. They are proud, obnoxious, selfish, angry, and lazy. Yet our children can be proud, obnoxious, selfish, angry, and lazy, and we still have affection for them. Obviously, ugly character need not stifle genuine love (which is good news for our own ugly hearts!). That's why hope is so powerful. It's not hope that their hearts will soon be less ugly. It's hope that even through that ugliness of heart God is painting a stunning portrait of *his* glory. And at its grand revealing, the astonished chorus of heaven will delight with a new degree of wonder at the perfections of our God.

Years ago, I found one man at my church to be particularly obnoxious and rude. Gavin seemed to go out of his way to find fault with me, often voicing his criticism to others.[10] I felt I was exhibiting plenty of the Spirit's power simply to tolerate him. Then came the day when he fell on hard times. He was in financial need, and I coordinated help from the congregation. He was in a rough spot in his marriage, and I was on the front lines of care. And you know what? I began to see his faith in a way I never had before.

10 For reasons you can well imagine, this is a highly disguised composite sketch of something I've experienced multiple times. At least at the time I'm writing this, there is no one in my church named Gavin.

I began to see how, by faith, he really struggled against what I'd faulted him for in the past—even though I couldn't perceive substantial progress. I began to see how much faith it took for him to receive care from me, far more than it took for me to provide that care. I saw in him a humility that I'd never noticed before. At first, that didn't mean much. After all, this was still critical, obnoxious Gavin. But as I came to appreciate his faith and considered what God was doing through it, something new began to grow in my heart. It was hope. My thoughts about him shifted from dread (What's Gavin going to do this time?) to hope (What's God doing in Gavin?). In that hope came real joy at God's hand in Gavin's life. And in that joy grew a genuine affection for him that I can honestly say I never expected to experience.

So in that person who disagrees with you so vehemently, do you see a commitment to conscience she never had before coming to Christ? That's a hopeful glimpse into the glory of Jesus. In that person who has terribly wrongheaded thoughts of how your church should respond to the social crisis of the day, do you see a desire for Christ to be honored? That's a hopeful glimpse into the glory of Jesus. What about that person who collects conspiracy theories like buried treasure? Do you see his growing desire to consider others when he speaks? That's a hopeful glimpse into the glory of Jesus.

Of course, like fine wine or modern art or the game of golf, this hope is an acquired taste. It's far from the usual consumeristic "What's in it for me?" mentality. We will grow in this affection-producing hope as we become practiced at keeping one eye on where these people are today and another on what they are becoming. That is, one eye focused on evidences of God's grace that we can see right now, while the eye other looks ahead with hope at the glory of God we know will one day be unveiled in them.

But what if we can't see *any* evidence of God's grace in "those people"? That brings us to the next phrase in Paul's triad.

"Be Patient in Tribulation"

This second phrase in Romans 12:12 also calls to mind Romans 5, where Paul says to rejoice not only in the hope of the glory of God, but also in sufferings (5:3). Why would you *rejoice* in suffering? Because suffering leads to endurance, which leads to character, which leads to hope (Rom. 5:3–4). In hope you rejoice that on the last day, God will be better known and enjoyed because of this hard providence you've gone through. It's through suffering, Peter says, that "the genuineness of your faith—more precious than gold that perishes though it is tested by fire—may be found to result in praise and glory and honor at the revelation of Jesus Christ" (1 Pet. 1:7). Suffering is a stage set for the greatest of good—the demonstration of the beauty and glory of God.

As such, Paul's command in Romans 12:12 to "be patient in tribulation" flows out of the command that just precedes it, to "rejoice in hope." Rejoice in the hope that God *will* succeed in his quest to glorify himself in your life, and you will be patient even in times of tribulation.

In Romans 5, it doesn't seem like Paul has any particular suffering in mind. But here in Romans 12, in this most relational of chapters, we should consider how we might be patient in tribulations caused by our life *together*. Be patient in the tribulations your brothers and sisters cause you. And be patient in the tribulations you must walk through with them.

Very often when we consider the failings and weaknesses of those around us, "hope" for our impatient hearts means "hope for change"; that is, hope that God will soon change them so that they won't be so difficult. But Paul's teaching here in Romans 12 means that your love can be grounded in a stronger hope than hope for change. If all that powers your patience with difficult people is the hope that God will change them in this life, then you'll often be disappointed, because God does not promise change according to your timetable. Of course, God is fully able to snap his fingers (metaphorically) to fix what bothers you about another person. He is able . . . yet he delays. Why? Because he has something better in mind. Trust God that even in the weakness and difficulty of others, he is painting a magnificent portrait of his glory, and pray that hope in his greater purposes will invest your love with patience. Hope in God's purposes is a much more solid foundation for patient love than hope for change.

As I noted earlier, both of these phrases—"rejoice in hope" and "be patient in tribulation"—are tightly bound up with hope in the glory of God. When we see glimpses of that glory in those around us, hope produces joy. When we don't, hope produces patience. If you want to build genuine friendships with others in your church, your love must look beyond them. Instead, look to the hope of what *Christ* is doing in them. In this regard, Timothy is our model. Paul describes him this way in Philippians 2:20–21: "For I have no one like him, who will be genuinely concerned for your welfare. For they all seek their own interests, not those of Jesus Christ." Train your affections on the interests of Jesus Christ—that he would be glorified— and on the certain hope that he is accomplishing this great end through those around you at church, and you will grow toward genuine love.

"Be Constant in Prayer"

Nothing I've described in this chapter is easy to do. It's no surprise then that Paul ends this triad with a call to prayer. Not just any prayer, though. Prayer that is constant, devoted, persistent. As Charles Spurgeon described Paul's prescription of joy and patience in this passage, "neither of these remedies can be taken into the soul except they be mixed with a draught of prayer. Joy and patience are curative essences, but they must be dropped into a glass full of supplication, and then they will be wonderfully efficient."[11] What should we pray for? Here are a few suggestions for your prayer life from this passage:

- Pray that God would work in your heart so that your love for others would be increasingly genuine: affectionate love, honoring love, zealous love.
- Pray that your joy in Christ would generate affection for his children.
- Pray that over time you would find increasing joy in the hope that God will one day be glorified through the work he's done in your heart.
- Pray that those you find difficult to love would also discover the joy that comes from hoping in the certainty of God's work in you.

---

11 Charles Spurgeon, "Constant, Instant, Expectant," vol. 25, *Metropolitan Tabernacle Pulpit*, preached on June 22, 1879, the Spurgeon Center, www.spurgeon.org.

- Pray that you would trust the good purposes God has in mind when he delays the resolution of suffering in your life and in the lives of others.
- Pray that God would bring to fruition the good things he has in mind in those delays.
- Pray that you would grow in patience through your hope in the glory of God.
- Pray that your church community would increasingly be characterized by these things as well.

Of course, some of the most unifying prayer is prayer *for* the ones who drive you crazy. Here John Newton's advice is apt: "As to your opponent, I wish, that, before you set pen to paper against him . . . you may commend him by earnest prayer to the Lord's teaching and blessing. This practice will have a direct tendency to conciliate your heart to love and pity him; and such a disposition will have a good influence upon every page you write."[12]

The Outworking of Genuine Love

It may surprise you that this chapter is almost over, and I haven't yet discussed what Paul says this genuine love will actually look like. That's because the real battle is with our mindset. But with the right mindset in place, we are ready for Paul's commands in Romans 12:13–16, where he calls us to give up ourselves for the good of our brothers and sisters. We should give up our money for them: "Contribute to the needs of the saints." We should give

---

12 John Newton, *The Works of John Newton* (Carlisle PA: Banner of Truth, 2015), 1:269.

up our rights for them: "Bless those who persecute you."[13] We should give up our privacy for them: "Seek to show hospitality." We should invest our hearts in them so that we rejoice when they rejoice and weep when they weep. We should give of our reputations, associating with those others might consider as "lowly" and beneath us.

The true value of these acts of service is what they proclaim about God. God doesn't need our money, after all. He owns the cattle on a thousand hills (Ps. 50:10). He doesn't need your home; he is building mansions in heaven (John 14:2). He doesn't need your heart; his is far better! And no matter how significant it may seem for you to lay down your rights or associate with those whom society believes are beneath you, it's nothing compared to Jesus, who—for you—left the glory of heaven for a reeking stable.

God doesn't need your acts of service, but they delight him when they show off the miracle he has worked in your heart. As the hope of what God is doing creates genuine love in your heart, your affection for those who are not easy to love will demonstrate his glory in a way that is profound.

Paul's Pathway to Genuine Love

In Romans 12:1–16, Paul describes a path we can walk from avoiding "those" people, to tolerating them, to genuine friend-

---

13 Many have puzzled over why a command that is seemingly regarding outsiders is placed in a list of commands that seem most applicable within the community of faith. As a result, some have interpreted all of verses 14–16 as pertaining to persecutors outside the church. Others have interpreted this "persecution" as poor treatment inside the church. What's clear is that just as in Jesus's teaching in Luke 6:27–28, which this command echoes, Paul is reminding us that following Jesus will often involve laying down our rights.

ship. It begins with amazement at the mercy of God so we might love with divine strength (Rom. 12:1). It helps us see that Christ's reputation rests on those we're tempted to disdain (12:2). It clears out the cobwebs of pride, trusting that we need all those whom God has put into our churches (12:3). Beyond that, it shows that we belong to them, and so they are worthy of our love (12:4–8). This genuine love (12:9)—this honoring, affectionate, and zealous love (12:10–11)—comes as we set our minds not on our brothers and sisters but on our hope that God is revealing his glory through them (12:12). It comes in response to prayer (Rom. 12:12). And it comes as we step forward in love (12:13–16). All this is especially true of those who are not easy to love and, through our genuine love for *them*, God gains special glory.

Yet what if people are "not easy to love" not simply because they're difficult, but because they've wronged you? What if they're "not easy to love" because they can't even agree with you that something is in fact wrong? That's when genuine love and affection would seem especially imperiled, which is where Paul takes us next.

Questions for Reflection and Discussion

1. Which of Paul's commands in Romans 12:9–16 seems especially intimidating for you?

2. How should hope in God's purposes for others in your church change why and how you love them?

3. What's the difference between hoping that God will change people (in this life) and hope in his purposes for them?

6

How Can I *Really* Forgive "Those" People?

Truth 6: Divine Justice Empowers Full Forgiveness

Repay no one evil for evil, but give thought to do what is honorable in the sight of all. If possible, so far as it depends on you, live peaceably with all. Beloved, never avenge yourselves, but leave it to the wrath of God, for it is written, "Vengeance is mine, I will repay, says the Lord."

ROMANS 12:17–19

When Forgiveness Seems to Fail

People in your church will sometimes sin against you, and your Christian duty is to forgive. As Jesus commands in Luke 6:37, "Forgive, and you will be forgiven." Yet too often, it seems that bitterness, anger, and resentment persist even after earnest attempts to forgive. For example, you've honestly forgiven someone in your church who sinned against you, but years later the relationship hasn't recovered. Or you've forgiven, but raging, angry thoughts still boil in your heart when you see that person. If our goal is to "live in harmony with one another" (Rom. 12:16), then the failure of forgiveness to secure legitimate peace and harmony is a real problem. After all, the peace Paul exhorts us toward is rich and vibrant, not the icy "peace" that too often characterizes relationships at church. In fact, this problem is especially prevalent at church because church is one of the few places where relationships are close enough to cause real hurt, yet the community is large enough that you're tempted to "deal with" strained relationships simply by avoiding them.

In a fallen world, it is not always possible for forgiveness to restore a broken relationship. Yet I'm convinced that far too often, the reason forgiveness fails to secure relational peace is not because reconciliation is impossible but because the "forgiveness" being offered is not full forgiveness. It is not full forgiveness because it has not adequately grappled with the injustice of forgiveness. And it has not adequately grappled with the injustice of forgiveness because it has not sufficiently internalized the justice of God. This is the argument I will make in this chapter, based on Jesus's teaching on loving our enemies in Luke 6 and Paul's commentary on that teaching in Romans 12. I'll illustrate with an unfortunate episode in the lives of Sam and Hector.

A Painful Betrayal

Hector was devastated. He'd just gotten off the phone with Sam, an elder at his church who'd mentored him for years. Sam told

Hector he'd been caught stealing money at work—a complicated scheme worth tens of thousands of dollars—and he'd be pleading guilty to felony charges. What's more, because he was an elder, he would confess this to the entire church on Sunday and resign as an elder. Hector wasn't prepared for any of this. Wasn't it Sam who was always reciting that verse in Proverbs 10: "Whoever walks in integrity walks securely, / but he who makes his ways crooked will be found out" (v. 9)? How could he have done this?

Hector was angry. He felt betrayed. It was like a trapdoor had just opened under his feet. After all, if he couldn't trust Sam, what about all that Sam had taught him? He felt embarrassed. Embarrassed for Sam, to be sure—but also embarrassed for himself, as one well known at church for looking up to Sam. Didn't Sam realize that his sin affected more than just himself?

But it was the question Sam asked at the end of the conversation that really caught Hector off guard. "Look, I'm sorry for all this. I know I've betrayed your trust. Will you forgive me?"

His brain somewhat numb, Hector stumbled for a moment. "Uh, yeah . . . of course, I forgive you." It seemed like the only appropriate thing to say. But what exactly did those words mean?

What Forgiveness Involves

You've probably been in Hector's shoes before. Someone at church sins against you, and it hurts. Really hurts. So now, being a follower of Jesus, you know you must forgive. To quote Jesus again, "Forgive, and you will be forgiven" (Luke 6:37). So, according to Scripture, what would it mean for Hector to forgive Sam? To answer that question, let's go back to Jesus's teaching from Luke 6 on loving our enemies. Just before his admonition to forgive in verse 37, he offers these famous words:

> But I say to you who hear, Love your enemies, do good to those who hate you, bless those who curse you, pray for those who abuse you. To one who strikes you on the cheek, offer the other also, and from one who takes away your cloak do not withhold your tunic either. (Luke 6:27–29)

Jesus's teaching here implies three commitments. When struck on the cheek, we are not to hit back. That is, we commit not to punish. Nor are we to walk away as if nothing happened. That is, we commit not to pretend. Instead, we turn the other cheek. We commit to do exactly the opposite of what justice would demand. Let's walk through each of these commitments and Paul's commentary on them in Romans 12. As we do, we'll see how God's justice enables a full forgiveness that radically transcends our own perceptions of justice and, as such, has radical power to restore peace.

Commitment 1: Forgiveness Does Not Punish

Romans 12:17 echoes Jesus's teaching: "Repay no one evil for evil, but give thought to do what is honorable in the sight of all." Sometimes that's easier said than done; a desire to punish threatens our efforts to forgive, as childish as that may sound. Someone criticizes you in front of others and you attack right back. Or for the more passive-aggressive, you might respond by slandering them. "You wouldn't *believe* what Anna said to me." Or you punish by letting an icy silence settle over the relationship.

This was certainly Hector's first, sinful impulse as soon as he ended the call. He wanted to call someone else at church to talk about what Sam had done. He pictured himself exploding back in anger at Sam. Hector thought (with some degree of sinful satisfaction) about the hurt Sam would feel when he realized what his sin had done to their friendship.

But whether through attack or slander or silence, punishment is wrong because it seizes a tool that's not ours to wield. This is Paul's point at the end of Romans 12. You might think of these verses as the theological foundation underneath Jesus's teaching to love our enemies (even those at church who at times can *feel* like enemies). Paul repeats Jesus's admonition (Rom. 12:14, 17), then moves on to explain *how* we can love like this. How can Hector refrain from punishing Sam in his thoughts, words, or actions?

God's Justice Is Necessary for Full Forgiveness

The principle Paul lays out is bracing at first; it seems so harsh that we might be embarrassed to admit it's behind our acts of forgiveness. Yet here it is: "Vengeance is mine, I will repay, says the Lord" (Rom. 12:19).

Forgiveness cannot be cavalier about justice. It's only because of God's commitment to justice that we can love our enemies (Luke 6:35) and forgive them (6:37). If you are to escape the desire to punish (which, for moral creatures who value justice, is an understandable desire), you must deliberately entrust yourself to the God who will avenge all wrong.

Thankfully, this is where Hector's thoughts went. He considered the example of Jesus in 1 Peter 2:23: "When he was reviled, he did not revile in return; when he suffered, he did not threaten, but continued entrusting himself to him who judges justly." For-giveness does not say, "This sin need not be punished." Rather, forgiveness says, "Because God punishes, it's not my place to punish." This means that forgiveness is either looking back to past justice or ahead to future justice. When we forgive someone who, as a Christian, has been forgiven by God, we are looking back to the justice God secured at the cross. When we forgive someone who is not in Christ, forgiveness looks ahead to justice that God will one day secure (hoping, of course, that this person does in fact turn to Christ). Empowered by God's promise of justice, forgiveness makes a very deliberate turn. It turns from the place of the judge to stand with the offender in love. This shift neces-sarily violates our sense of fairness. And this shift is critical: unless we deliberately choose to hold onto *God's* promise of justice, our earnest attempts at forgiveness will often collapse under the weight of justice denied. Absent God's promise of justice, forgiveness cannot be as radically unfair as it really must be.

The False Promise of Anger

Hector resolved to refrain from punishment in action, word, or even in thought, a resolution that found power in God's promise to secure justice. After all, *God* was the one who would deal with Sam's sin. In fact, since Sam was a Christian God had *already* done that—at the cross. Securing justice wasn't Hector's job. But what was he to do with the anger he still felt at Sam?

This is where Hector—like so many of us when we're wronged—needed to hear James's words about anger: "Let every person be quick to hear, slow to speak, slow to anger; for the anger of man does not produce the righteousness of God" (James 1:19–20).

Anger *can* be wonderfully beneficial, supplying courage to fight for what's right. For fallen creatures, anger frequently motivates a wrong desire to punish, which is why James warns us. When you're blistering with anger, all your friends see is your anger. But what *you* feel is injustice, and your desire for righteousness. Yet James tells you that the promises anger makes to secure righteousness are frequently false promises. The response of punishment that anger encourages will not accomplish justice, because only God can accomplish justice. "The anger of man does not produce the righteousness of God" (James 1:20).

Hector was wise to observe his anger, but he was also wise not to obey his anger, doing what it was telling him to do. By observing his anger, he could see that he still had work to do to entrust the injustice of the situation to God. That was helpful. But he'd learned long ago to be skeptical of obeying his anger, because anger almost always promises a righteousness it cannot deliver.

Commitment 2: Forgiveness Does Not Pretend

Yet Hector couldn't stop with simply refraining from punishment. Surely forgiveness must seek to close the open wound that now separated him from Sam. How would that happen? Hector thought of 1 Corinthians 13:5, love "keeps no record of wrongs" (NIV). Perhaps the best way forward would be to treat Sam as if this sin had never happened. Hector would do his best to simply erase the whole affair from his memory.

But Hector's strategy is better described as pretending than forgiving. Pretending may seem to be the easier path, and it is certainly more socially acceptable than blowing up in anger. But pretending is not forgiveness. I appreciate how Alasdair Groves puts it: "The heart of the self-protective withdrawer is not more righteous than the aggressive engager."[1] When we pretend that no wrong was done, our attempts at "forgiveness" often buckle under the weight of the continued injustice we feel.

As time went on, Hector realized that this was exactly his situation. He felt his face flush when Sam wanted to talk with him. He found himself second-guessing the sincerity of Sam's words. Pretending that the incident never happened was clearly not working.

Consider, however, how often we *do* confuse pretending with forgiveness—even in the words we use to "forgive." "Oh, it was nothing." "Don't worry about it." "No big deal." "No harm, no foul." Statements like these deny the injustice of the offense, which in turn undermines the injustice that forgiveness requires. C. S. Lewis puts this well, "Real forgiveness means looking steadily at the sin, the sin that is left over without any excuse, after all allowances have been made, and seeing it in all its horror, dirt, meanness and malice, and nevertheless being wholly reconciled to the man who has done it. That, and only that, is forgiveness."[2]

If a church is to reflect the unity and beauty of God's perfect character, we cannot settle for the false forgiveness of pretending. And remember: real forgiveness will often feel unjust because it replaces the punishment that justice demands with an obligation to love.[3]

---

1   Alasdair Groves and Myriam Hertzog, "Anger Management," September 5, 2018, in *Where Life and Scripture Meet*, produced by CCEF, podcast, https://www.ccef.org/podcast/.

2   C. S. Lewis, "On Forgiveness," in *Fern-Seed and Elephants and Other Essays on Christianity*, ed. Walter Hooper (Glasgow: Fount Paperbacks, 1975), 42.

3   The fact that God *requires* forgiveness (meaning it is wrong to not forgive) in no way eliminates the way in which forgiveness feels like a violation of our God-given sense of justice.

We saw earlier that God's promise of vengeance in Romans 12 protects us from punishing. It also protects us from pretending. That's because it reminds us that justice matters. It matters to God, and it should matter to us. Only when we look justice square in the face and entrust it to God can we fully and deliberately embrace all the glorious *in*justice of forgiveness.

The Danger of Bitterness

This is how we avoid the pitfall of bitterness. Bitterness is the corrosive residue that remains when we feel that justice was denied. You know that wrong was done, you know that justice was not done, your heart cries out for justice, and bitterness ensues. To escape bitterness, forgiveness must cling to God's promise of justice. And it must entrust to God not only the judicial consequences of sin but its circumstantial and relational consequences as well. That is, you must believe that *every* hardship—even every sin against you—is part of God's plan to do you good (Heb. 12:10–11).

A Painful Conversation

All this came to a head one Sunday as Hector looked at Sam across the room and felt his insides boil. "If I were a more mature Christian, maybe this wouldn't bother me so much. But clearly it does. I need to talk with him." So Hector arranged for a good time to speak with Sam. He explained how deeply Sam's sin had hurt him, the sense of betrayal he felt, the ways it had challenged his trust in the other elders—and even in God. But the conversation did not go well. At first, Sam was apologetic. "Yes, I know that I hurt you. That's why I called to tell you before the whole church found out." But as they continued to talk, Sam grew less sympathetic. "Look, Hector, I'm sorry you were hurt. But I've got bigger things on my plate right now. I've lost my job and with this on my record I'm having a hard time finding another. It's taking a toll on my marriage. I don't feel I have any real friendships at church anymore; I'm just the 'disgraced elder.' Do you think you could just lay off and let bygones be bygones?"

So what is Hector to do now?

Commitment 3: Forgiveness Pays the Cost

Hector's situation isn't unusual. After all, it's rare that someone really understands the depth of their offense against you. Instead of seeing this roadblock as the end of forgiveness, Hector must now venture further into the injustice of forgiveness. Remember, this is what Jesus described. Were someone to strike you on the cheek, punishment would be to hit back. Pretending would act as if the offense didn't matter. But Jesus says to do neither. Instead, he tells us to "offer the other also." In response to your rights being violated, forgiveness would have you lay down your rights.

Every offense has consequences. Though Jesus paid Sam's punishment, temporal consequences of his sin remain, as Hector is discovering. Sometimes those consequences are small. Sometimes they are significant. Real forgiveness lays down its rights and says, "I will come alongside you to repair what's been broken as if it were my fault."

This is implicit in the very language Jesus uses to describe forgiveness. Think for a moment of his parable in Matthew 18:21–35 of two servants who owe a debt to their master. In Jesus's story, it's the *forgiver* who pays the debt. The same is true for you. You, the offended one, pay the debt. There's no such thing as cheap forgiveness. You leave your position facing off against the offender and walk around to his side. "I'm going to work with you to build this back, as if this sin were mine." This is so contrary to a false forgiveness that says, "I won't hold this against you, but you'd better grovel your way back into my good graces." Ken Sande states this well.

> Forgiveness can be a costly activity. When you cancel a debt, it does not simply disappear. Instead, you absorb a liability that someone else deserves to pay. Similarly, forgiveness requires that you absorb certain effects of another person's sins and you release that person from liability to punishment. This is precisely what Christ accomplished on Calvary.[4]

How often have we failed to extend full forgiveness because we have assumed it would not cost us very much? Even the oft-repeated advice to "first forgive yourself" reveals how we have psychologized a concept that is at its core judicial, feeding our delusion that forgiveness comes without cost.

So what does it look like for forgiveness to bear the cost of the offense? Sometimes—especially for smaller offenses, this means overlooking the offense. As Proverbs 19:11 says, "Good sense makes one slow to anger, / and it is his glory to overlook an offense." When an offense does not pose an ongoing danger to you or to the offender, and it is small enough that you can overlook it without danger to the relationship, it is your "glory" to overlook an offense.

---

4 Ken Sande, *The Peacemaker* (Grand Rapids, MI: Baker, 1997), 188.

However, for offenses that are more significant, absorbing the consequences of the offense will often be more costly. This might mean bearing the tangible, physical costs of a sin—like footing the repair bill yourself when a friend carelessly damaged something they borrowed. More often, forgiveness is less about bearing physical consequences and more about relational consequences. For example, an offense destroys trust. Trust must be rebuilt. Yet forgiveness does not stand back, waiting for the offender to earn trust back. Instead, as Paul says in Romans 12:20, it leans forward in love. In forgiveness, you come alongside that person and take on the risk of helping him regain your trust. Or perhaps an offense destroys affection and warmth in your relationship. Instead of sitting back and making her pursue you, you pursue *her*, offering the time that's necessary to rebuild what was lost. Forgiveness accepts the consequences of the offense as your own to bear, laying down your rights in order to restore what was lost. And forgiveness says, "I will not resent taking this on because Christ did not resent taking it on for me."

Forgiveness Is Anti-Fair

Yet it feels unfair, even wrong, to respond to injustice this way. How many times have you explained forgiveness to a child only to hear, "But that's not fair!" Of course. That's the whole point. Yet it must be noted that forgiveness is not *merely* unfair. After all, partial forgiveness that refrains from punishment yet stands there, arms crossed, refusing to go further—such partial forgiveness could also be called unfair, couldn't it? Partial forgiveness feels virtuous because you're not giving them *all* the punishment they deserve. Yet biblical forgiveness goes further. We're not merely to refrain from striking back; we're to offer the other cheek also. To give the opposite of what justice demands. Calling such a forgiveness "unfair" is an understatement. Perhaps "anti-fair" better captures the glorious reversal of justice that Jesus describes.

Does this sound extreme? It should. How can a forgiveness that's rooted in loving even our *enemies* be anything but extreme? So how can we forgive like this? How can we embrace the "anti-fair" ethic of forgiveness, absorbing the cost of the offense, so that we respond in love? In short, we do this because Christ has forgiven us. As Paul writes to the Colossians, "*As the Lord has forgiven you*, so you also *must* forgive" (3:13). It is Christ's forgiveness of you that completes the "anti-fair" reversal of justice that forgiveness must entail. The reality of God's wrath removes vengeance from your hands; the reality that God's wrath fell on Christ rather than on you replaces it with the obligation to love. In that sense, we must remember that the principles in this book build on each other, just as Paul's do in the book of Romans. We cannot simply jump in and expect to muster up this radical, "anti-fair" forgiveness. Rather, we must depend on the mercy we've received from Christ (Rom. 12:1), cherishing *his* reputation (12:2), abandoning the pride that says we'd be better off without those who offend us (12:3–8), clinging to the hope of what God is doing (12:9–13). Only then can we can embrace the anti-fair ethic of full forgiveness.

Even When They Don't "Get It"

Yet there's another wrinkle we must consider, another barrier to restoring broken relationships in the church. Very often, those who have offended against you *have no idea* what the offense really did to you. This is Hector's position, isn't it? So often, this is the missing ingredient that keeps a conflict burning even after honest attempts at forgiveness. "He just doesn't get it." "She has no idea what she did to me."

Incidentally, this is why we should always attempt to articulate the cost of our sin when we apologize. Don't just say "I'm sorry I spoke behind your back to Joe, that was gossip; please forgive me." To be sure, naming your sin with biblical language like "gossip" is a good and humbling start, but it's insufficient. Instead: "Please forgive me for gossiping about you; I know how much you respect Joe, and I see how my words have hurt your reputation with him." As best you can, articulate what your sin cost the one you offended, and invite him to fill in what you don't yet see.

Yet no matter how well offenders acknowledge the consequences of their sin, they will never "get it." They will never know as well as you do what they took from you. But *God* knows. And that is critical. He's seen all that was done. The fact that God will exact justice for this offense—and moreover, that for the Christian he will exact justice from his own Son—tells us he is intimately acquainted with the cost of forgiveness. *He* "gets it."

Partial forgiveness makes earnest commitments while struggling that the offender doesn't "get it." Complete forgiveness entrusts justice to God, confident that he knows exactly what forgiveness will cost.

Paying the Cost

Hector struggled with that passage about turning the other cheek. At times, Jesus's teaching seems so extreme, it's difficult to know what to do with it. If you're carjacked, are you really to say, "Wait, let me go around the corner and get my other car as well"?[5] But this time, what Jesus said really resonated with Hector. He thought, "Turning the other cheek means giving an offender the opposite of what he deserves. Forgiveness means giving Sam the opposite of what he deserves. What would that be?"

Ideas flooded into Hector's head. Sam didn't deserve Hector's friendship—not after what he did at work, and certainly not after how he responded to Hector. The opposite of that would be to pursue Sam in friendship, if Sam were still interested. Sam didn't deserve Hector's trust either. Of course, Hector couldn't simply snap his fingers and start trusting Sam again. But he could give Sam opportunities to rebuild trust. Finally, Sam didn't deserve Hector's respect. This was perhaps the hardest load of all for Sam to bear since he was accustomed to being respected at church. Again, Hector couldn't simply *decide* to respect Sam. But he could watch for opportunities to rebuild that aspect of their relationship, seeking Sam's advice where he *could* trust Sam. Above all, Hector could commit to serve Sam by praying for him regularly.

Hector determined to love Sam in this way, seeking to embrace the anti-fair ethic of forgiveness. I wish I could give you a happy ending, where Sam once again ministers to Hector the way he used to and Hector and Sam are best buddies. Sadly, in a fallen world things rarely work out that way. But even in stories with imperfect endings, the love that Paul and Jesus describe has a way

5 We must understand Jesus's teaching in Luke 6 that Paul repeats in Romans 12 in light of Paul's teaching on the God-ordained authority of government to punish wrongdoing in Romans 13.

of softening angry hearts. As Hector has made it a point to pray regularly for Sam, his own heart has changed toward this brother in Christ. He's begun to realize that some of his anger was rooted in a self-righteous failure to approach Sam with the grace he's received from Christ. And Sam has appreciated Hector's periodic invitations to get breakfast at a local diner and his text messages asking how he can pray. Sam and Hector may never agree on the harm Sam's sin did to Hector, but that doesn't necessarily mean that full forgiveness can't create a peace between them that is real, vibrant, and rich. Reconciliation isn't always possible; God never makes that promise. But so often we settle for something so much less, thinking that it's the best we can do, when in fact what we call "forgiveness" has not embraced the anti-fair ethic of Christian love.

Our Forgiveness Reflects Christ's Forgiveness

Forgiveness is a significant way in which our relationships at church reflect the glory of God. That's the reason Jesus gave when he told us to love our enemies in Luke 6:35–36:

> "And your reward will be great [God sees what this is costing you, and he will not forget], and you will be sons of the Most High [as a child representing your Father, you are showing off his bountiful love for us], for he is kind to the ungrateful and the evil [remember, that was you]. Be merciful, even as your Father is merciful."

Your church was designed to reflect Jesus's perfect character, so you can take pleasure knowing that your forgiveness is demonstrating the depth of his.

Do your attempts at forgiveness fail to secure peace? Then prayerfully work your way through these four questions. (1) Has your forgiveness left behind all desire to punish? (2) Have you pretended that no offense was committed instead of doing the hard work of forgiving? (3) In forgiveness, have you committed to taking on yourself the consequences of the offense? (4) Have you made efforts to pursue the offender in love? Entrust justice to God so that, far from being overcome by evil, you will overcome evil with good (Rom. 12:21).

Notice as we've made our way through Romans 12 how the situations Paul addresses have become more morally charged. He first broached the topic of right and wrong in 12:9 with the evil of hypocritical love. Romans 12:14 described how we should respond when we're wronged ("bless those who persecute you"). And now in these final verses of Romans 12, moral language is on full display as Paul points us to the vengeance of God. This is significant. Love is hard enough when it's simply our preferences and opinions that are at stake. But once issues of right and wrong enter the picture, love reaches a whole new degree of difficulty. That forces us to dig deep into the justice of God, an attribute that we don't consider often enough. Yet Paul has one further hurdle for us to consider. What if we can't even agree with others on *whether* something is wrong? That brings us to two final truths we must consider if we are to love the ones who drive us crazy.

Questions for Reflection and Discussion

1. Which pitfalls do you more often stumble into: seeking to punish those who have wronged you, attempting to pretend that no wrong was done, or something else?

2. Why is it important that our forgiveness be not merely *un*fair but *anti*-fair?

3. Where does your church do well in extending forgiveness? Where does it struggle?

Prayer Points

- Pray that you would recognize where your attempts at forgiveness are falling short of what Scripture calls you to.
- Pray that your congregation would be characterized by forgiveness that reflects the forgiveness they've received through Christ.
- Pray that your church's leaders would be quick to forgive each other.

7

How Can I Stop Judging and Despising "Those" People?

Truth 7: People You Dislike Often Act in Faith

The one who eats, eats in honor of the Lord, since he gives thanks to God, while the one who abstains, abstains in honor of the Lord and gives thanks to God. For none of us lives to himself, and none of us dies to himself.

ROMANS 14:6–7

Disagreement Over Right and Wrong

For Grace, the pandemic was gut-wrenching. It was inconvenient to be sure, with shutdowns, restrictions, and cancelled plans. Beyond that, as a socially minded citizen it was challenging to watch many of her neighbors disregard public health restrictions that she felt were perfectly reasonable. But most of all it was agonizing for her as a Christian because the opinions she despised in society were also present in her church. How could she go to church with people who didn't take the pandemic seriously? For Grace, church became an exceedingly difficult place. In fact, far from a time to worship, Sunday mornings were increasingly a time for her to stew in anger, brooding over that person to her left who was disobeying the government's mask order, or that person in front of her who'd told her the whole thing was a hoax.

The challenge for Grace wasn't simply the fact that she disagreed with other members of her church. It was the moral dimension of this disagreement. The thoughts attacking her on Sunday mornings weren't merely "Hey, I wish you'd put a mask on" but "What you're doing is *wrong*. How can you behave that way and claim to follow Christ?" All this was fertile ground for feelings of judging, despising, and even loathing in her heart. And this put Grace in some perilous spiritual territory.

Sadly, all of this became far more challenging—and more real—the morning she was awakened by a frantic call from her mom. Her beloved uncle, whom she had gone hiking with just two weeks before, was in the ICU with the virus, fighting for his life.

Put yourself in her shoes. What do you do when the same ideas that have harmed those you love are embraced by some in your church? Ideas have consequences, a reality that amplifies the moral issues at stake and creates the perfect conditions for division in a church. You lose your job because you won't give in to the transgender agenda, while some in your church belittle your concerns as unnecessary "culture wars." Your family was pulled out of poverty by civil rights legislation while some in your church teach their kids that the whole movement was nothing more than a left-wing power grab.

Of course, the idea that we'd disagree with others at church over what's right and what's wrong is nothing new. Having written in Romans 12 about sacrificial love within the church, and having taken a brief detour to address some related questions about government, Paul turns in Romans 14 to address this moral dimension of disagreement. There, he warns us of two sins that can emerge amidst convictional conflict.

The first is *despising* other Christians for the convictions they hold. In Romans 14, this is the sin of the more permissive crowd. Addressing the question of whether Christians are permitted to eat certain foods, Paul writes that the one who eats must not "despise the one who abstains" (14:3). Despising one another has no place in God's church. Even if your position is correct.

The second trap is *judging* one another. That is, declaring someone guilty for actions that aren't demonstrably sinful—either because they're sins of the heart (like pride) or actions Scripture doesn't explicitly condemn (like drinking wine). We are so good at judging others, aren't we? Just scroll through social media (or the texts on your own phone) to see a thousand variants on the phrase "How *could* they?" Indignation feels so good. Outrage feels righteous. Yet on matters where Christians can legitimately disagree, Paul says, any judging that pushes others away has no place in God's church. Even if your position is correct.

Consider these four questions from this section of Romans to reveal when you are wrongly judging or despising others.

1. Do you look down on this person? Has it become difficult to honor this person in your words and actions as Paul commands in Romans 12:10?

2. Do you find yourself *assuming* that someone's motives are ungodly? That's the heart of judging (14:3–4).

3. Do you care more about winning the disagreement than you do about the good of the person disagreeing with you? (14:20–22).

4. Do you find that your affection for this person has been damaged (Rom. 12:10)? Waning affection is often the first sign that something has gone wrong in your heart.

Differences in conviction don't necessarily damage church unity. But judging and despising do. It's insightful that Paul describes the opposite of despising and judging as "welcoming" those we disagree with (14:1; 15:7), which reveals the relational consequences of these sins. Judging and despising distance us from one another through perceived inferiority; welcoming draws us into friendship because of fellowship in Christ.

Caught in the Trap

Yet abandoning these attitudes is easier said than done. Judging and despising are sins of the heart. You can't decide to stop judging and despising any more than you can decide to stop your cancer, because both are within you. Someone says, "I *know* that I'm to 'welcome' that person. I *know* that I'm to 'not quarrel over opinions (Rom. 14:1).' But I still feel anger and resentment rising in my heart. What can I do?"

This is exactly what Grace was feeling as she sat in church, her heart steaming with anger. She decided months ago that she wouldn't let disagreements over pandemic restrictions push her out of her church. After all, she thought, "If *these* issues don't fall into the realm of Christian freedom, what does?" She knew that her judgmental, angry thoughts were sinful and displeasing to God. Surely God didn't want her coming to church simply to sit there despising others in her heart. But she felt trapped.

Do you recognize these sins in your own life? Remember that we're often simultaneously guilty of both judging *and* despising. You send your kids to public school, secretly despising a family who, you're quite sure, has stopped giving to the church so they can pay tuition at a Christian school. Can't they see that public school isn't the immoral monster they make it out to be? You're despising the one with a stricter conscience. *At the same time*, your heart judges another family who misses church every few weeks because of their daughter's travel soccer team. Now you're judging the one who acts with more freedom. The fact that this judging and despising are wrong doesn't mean that there's no truth to your concerns about either family. But such a posture could hardly be called love.

So what are you going to do? After his famous words, "Judge not, and you will not be judged" (Luke 6:37), Jesus tells you to "take the log out of your own eye, and then you will see clearly to take out the speck that is in your brother's eye" (6:42). How do you remove the log of judging and despising?

See Their Faith

For Grace, a turning point came at the most unexpected time. As the pandemic ebbed, her church held a congregational meeting to discuss loosening restrictions. Near the end of the meeting, a woman named Serena stood up.

Over the past few months, Serena had been having a very different struggle than Grace. Though initially open to reasonable public health measures, she felt as time wore on that the medicine was becoming worse than the disease. For her church in particular, restrictions on congregational life were being measured in struggling marriages, strained friendships, battered faith, and even fractured church unity. With that, her patience had worn thin for church pandemic policies that insisted on following or even exceeding government restrictions that themselves had dangerously overreached. That struggle compounded when the church announced in the early (chilly) spring that once again they'd be meeting outdoors. Yet as church members who saw things similarly came to her to complain, she'd pled with them not give up on church and to continue to trust their leaders. Like Grace, she too was determined that pandemic restrictions would not push her out of the church she loved.

As Serena stood up, then, it was with anguish—and anger—that she described how difficult the church's decision to return to meeting outdoors had been for her, for her family, and for so many others. It was difficult to accept that her church had gone along with a government response that in her mind had been wildly overblown. Serena was exactly the kind of person Grace had struggled to love.

Yet it was Serena's outpouring of emotion at that congregational meeting that shook something loose in Grace's angry heart. As Grace described later, "It was seeing her pain—the same pain I was feeling—even though we were coming from opposite sides of the issue. It was seeing in her tears the same love of this church that I had, the same faith that I had—even though we couldn't disagree more about what our church should do." It was seeing her own pain and her own faith reflected in someone she disagreed with that began the process of rooting out these sins from Grace's heart. "I knew on a theoretical level that someone could disagree with me and still be a Christian. But Serena was living proof. What I needed wasn't a theory; I needed a person. A person whose faith was real, and whose faith was driving her heart—even if on this issue her heart was pointed in the opposite direction as mine."

Seeing the faith of those we disagree with is, in fact, a key prescription in Romans 14 for those struggling with judging and despising. In verse 3, Paul shames us for pushing away those whom God has already welcomed. And why has God welcomed them? Why will they "stand" under his judgment (14:4)? Through faith in Christ. Very often, people on *both* sides of a debate are motivated by sincere faith, and that's a truth we must internalize if we're to love well.

> One person esteems one day as better than another, while another esteems all days alike. Each one should be fully convinced in his own mind. The one who observes the day, observes it in honor of the Lord. The one who eats, eats in honor of the Lord, since he gives thanks to God, while the one who abstains, abstains in honor of the Lord and gives thanks to God. For none of us lives to himself, and none of us dies to himself. (Rom. 14:5–7)

Both sides seek to honor the Lord. Both sides are living for Christ and not for themselves. And so both sides are acting in faith.

We often presume the worst of motives in those we disagree with. That suggests that only evil motives could lead someone to look at the same facts we do and arrive at a different conviction. But godly people frequently look at the same facts and come to different convictions.

We're often told to "assume the best" (see 1 Cor. 13:7). And yet, assuming the best is only the doorway to doing what Paul encourages here in Romans 14. Assume the best, yes—and then walk through that door to explore and understand what really motivates this Christian on the other side. Don't stop with assuming—even if you're assuming good. Find out. Find out how real faith and a real desire to honor Christ can motivate opinions that are the opposite of your own. Sometimes you'll be disappointed, discovering that someone's motives really are as bad as you feared. But at least then you won't be naïvely "assuming the best" about something that's false. Yet very often, if these are real Christians we're talking about, you'll discover real faith. While that discovery is unlikely to resolve a disagreement, it can do wonders for your judging and despising.

"I just don't understand how anyone could *ever* be part of my church and believe that." Does that thought ever cross your mind? When it does, you must choose to see it not as a rhetorical punchline, but as the beginning of a conversation. What Paul describes here—seeing their faith—is the goal of that conversation. Don't sit back and judge. Talk. And when you talk, don't be content with merely understanding their convictions. Don't even be content with understanding the experiences that have shaped those convictions. Understand the faith that drives them. Here are some ideas for just such a conversation:

- Ask how their faith motivates the opinion you disagree with. To use Grace and Serena as an example, Grace might ask, "What biblical principles have shaped how you think our church should navigate the pandemic?"

- Ask how their faith leads to a different prioritization of values than your own. "It seems that you value unrestricted church gatherings above public health. To me, that seems to push against Jesus's command to love our neighbors. What do you think I'm missing?"
- Ask how their faith has changed their thinking over time. "As the pandemic has progressed, how has your desire to honor Christ changed what you're most concerned about?"

There's a destructive spiral of suspicion we must be wary of at church. You're skeptical of a person's motives, which leads you to misinterpret his words and actions, which leads you to be more suspicious of his motives, and so forth. "Seeing their faith" is how you break the cycle. This is yet another example of putting on those 3-D "faith glasses" I described earlier. Without them, all you see is confused disagreement and conflict. But pop those glasses on, and suddenly a whole new dimension appears—the dimension of faith. Suddenly, you see the beauty of God's hand at work, with divergent opinions growing out of a common faith in the goodness of God, and a common desire to honor God.

Only Half the Problem

See the faith of those you disagree with. For Grace this was exactly what she needed, and God used Serena's faith to quiet the raging of Grace's judgmental heart. Yet can't this conceivably cross into moral relativism, where unity trumps all disagreement? For example, what if Grace was living in Chicago in the 1960s and her concern was over White members of her church working to evict a new neighbor simply because he's Black? Does Paul's advice in

Romans 14 mean that by seeing the faith of those who repress non-Whites, she should turn a blind eye to these evils? That's where we must consider a final truth in these closing chapters of Romans: the judgment of God.

Questions for Reflection and Discussion

1. Do you think you're more prone to judging others (in Rom. 14, the sin of the more restrictive conscience) or despising others (the sin of the freer conscience)?

2. Can you think of a time when, like Grace, you saw how someone's conviction that opposed your own was motivated by faith? How did that change your attitude toward that person?

3. How can we follow Paul's advice in Romans 14:5–8 to consider the faith-filled motivations of those we disagree with without falling into the trap of moral relativism?

Prayer Points

- Pray that you would be obedient to your conscience and also loving and charitable toward those who arrive at different convictions.
- Pray that your congregation would be known for welcoming even those in the church they disagree with (Rom. 14:1; 15:7).
- Pray that your church leaders would be wise in discerning which differences of conscience are within the realm of Christian freedom.

8

How Can I Love "Those"
People When They're Wrong?

Truth 8: We Will Answer to God

Why do you pass judgment on your brother?
Or you, why do you despise your brother? For we
will all stand before the judgment seat of God.

ROMANS 14:10

Just a Few Extra Verses, Please

Have you ever wondered why Scripture isn't more clear on some issues? If the Holy Spirit knew that disagreements over the end times would divide the church (and he did), surely he could have thrown in a verse that says, "You have heard it said that the millennium isn't a literal thousand years, but I say to you that it is and, by the way, it will precede Christ's return." Wouldn't that

125

little addition have saved us a whole mess of trouble? If the "eating meat" controversies get *two* passages of Scripture (Rom. 14; 1 Cor. 8), couldn't we have a bit more nuance on, say, when Christians should disobey the government and how we should address the injustices of our ancestors?

Yet when Paul says that Scripture is the "*whole* counsel of God" (Acts 20:27), and when he tells Timothy that it makes us "complete, equipped for *every* good work" (2 Tim. 3:17), he's saying that God got the Bible exactly right. As the Belgic Confession puts it, Scripture provides "as much as we need in this life, for God's glory and for our salvation."[1] That's true for the detail the Spirit gave us in Scripture and it's also true for the details he withheld. Where we disagree, the problem lies with us and not with God's perfect word—and yet even the disagreements that arise from our sins and imperfections are not outside the control of a sovereign God.

This is, after all, the backdrop behind Romans 14:1–15:7 that we began looking at in the previous chapter. The "opinions" (14:1) Paul addresses are disputed because Scripture isn't as clear as these believers may have wished. Yet rather than calling on them to settle their disagreements, he tells them to love one another *despite* such disagreement. The result? Romans 15:6: "Together you may with one voice glorify the God and Father of our Lord Jesus Christ." Differences in conviction, yes. Differences in conscience, yes. Yet it's precisely *because of* those differences that God gets glory through their insistence on unity in Christ.

As you face differences of conviction that could tear your church apart, the Holy Spirit isn't regretting that he didn't pro-

---

1   Belgic Confession, article 2.

vide more clarity in Scripture. These differences are *opportunities* to demonstrate that being "in accord with Christ Jesus" is all we need to be in "harmony with one another" (Rom. 15:5). That's how "with one voice" we "glorify the God and Father of our Lord Jesus Christ" (15:6). Remember, just as God gets greater glory through redemption than through creation alone, the glory he gets in your church's unity is greater in disagreement than if everyone had the same answer in the first place.

The "Problem" of Conviction

Yet that's easier said than done. Paul told us in Romans 12:9 to "abhor what is evil; hold fast to what is good." But what happens when we disagree on what's "evil" and what's "good?" It's one thing for a church to disagree on the color of carpeting. It's quite another to disagree over whether a Christian can cast a vote for a political candidate who downplays the ongoing consequences of racism. Or whether Christians may assent to an adoption agency's prohibition against physical discipline. Or whether a Christian can attend the celebration of a Hindu festival. What makes these disagreements so difficult is that for many, they are matters of right and wrong, not merely of preference. In the previous chapter, we discussed how we can stop judging and despising people. But how can we positively *love* them? J. C. Ryle wrote that "every man has a conscience within him, which must be satisfied before he can be truly happy."[2] That's true of my conscience, but it's also true of yours. If you're my friend and you're doing something against my conscience, your

2 J. C. Ryle, *Holiness: Its Nature, Hindrances, Difficulties and Roots* (London: William Hunt and Company, 1889), 364.

actions challenge my happiness and, as a result, they challenge our friendship.

Theoretically, we *could* just have different churches for different convictions. A church over here that's about the gospel *and* that speaks strongly about illegal immigration. A church over there that's about the gospel *and* that advocates for the payment of reparations to the descendants of slaves. Many years ago, while I was on a trip to Afghanistan, an article was published about the Kabul synagogue. Who knew there was still a synagogue in Kabul! But there was, though its membership was reduced to two men. And they made the news because, due to incessant quarrelling, they were considering splitting into *two* synagogues, each with a membership of one. Is this not where the "different churches for different convictions" takes us? Surely, we can do better.

And yet . . . can you really go to church with other Christians who are *wrong* on important matters? Can your attitude toward them really be the "genuine love" that Paul commands? That's what we'll address in this chapter. But first, we must understand exactly what type of disagreements we're talking about.

Different Speeds of Disagreement

As you'll recall, Paul begins Romans 14 by warning us not "to quarrel over opinions." The word the ESV translates as "opinions" literally means "reasonings"—consistent with its use here as reason-based implications of Scripture. Thus, the NIV uses the phrase "disputable matters." These disagreements are not about truths "either expressly set down in Scripture, or [that] by good and necessary consequence may be deduced from Scripture," to use the helpful language of the Westminster Confession.[3] Instead, they're based on reasoning *from* those truths. About such matters we should not quarrel.

Where does this fit into the broader hierarchy of disagreements we might have with fellow Christians? In their book *Conscience*, Andy Naselli and J. D. Crowley identify three different levels of disagreements.

- First-level disagreements are those one cannot deny "and still be a Christian in any meaningful sense."[4] These truths emerge as inescapable conclusions when the Scriptures are faithfully read, either because they are explicit in the text or rise unavoidably from the text.[5]
- Second-level disagreements "create reasonable boundaries between Christians."[6] These are issues faithful Christians may disagree on, and where disagreement means they should gather into different churches. Historically, disagreements over baptism and church government fall into this category.[7]

3   Westminster Confession of Faith, 1.6.

4   Andrew Naselli and J. D. Crowley, *Conscience: What It Is, How to Train It, and Loving Those Who Differ* (Wheaton, Illinois: Crossway, 2016), 86.

5   See Jonty Rhodes, "By Good and Necessary Consequence," *Tabletalk*, January 7, 2021, https://tabletalkmagazine.com/.

6   Naselli and Crowley, *Conscience*, 86.

7   One might ask, "Why would disagreements about baptism constitute 'reasonable boundaries between Christians' but not disagreements over issues like politics?" It should be observed that some Christians *don't* believe that churches should divide over baptism (e.g., the church I grew up in) and sometimes Christians *do* need to divide over politics (e.g., the Confessing Church in Nazi Germany). In general, however, we must note that disagreements over baptism are disagreements over *what* Jesus commands (Does the command to baptize mean we baptize infants or not?) whereas disagreements

129

- Third-level disagreements need not separate Christians into different churches. When I have referred to "nonessential" matters in this book, it is this category I have had in mind. That is, matters that are not essential to agree on to be together in a church.[8]

It's these third-level issues that Paul writes about in Romans 14. Specifically, he addresses three different disagreements, though he clearly intends the principles he lays out to apply more broadly. First is the question of whether a Christian can eat meat (14:2).[9] Next is a debate about celebrating special days (14:5).[10] And third was disagreement over Christians drinking wine (14:21). Of course, your church has its own set of disagreements. You may not *want* to be in church with people who disagree with you in these ways, but neither can you honestly say that these issues should split you into different churches.

---

over politics are normally disagreements over *how* to obey agreed-upon commands (Does the command to love your neighbor imply a balanced budget amendment or not?). For more nuance and detail on this question, see Jonathan Leeman, *How the Nations Rage* (Nashville, TN: Thomas Nelson, 2020).

8 It must be noted that "nonessential" does not mean "unimportant." One mistake modern Christians often make is to believe that whatever is nonessential for salvation is necessarily unimportant. The mirror-image pitfall of this tendency can lead Christians to unnecessarily divide churches because they assume that anything that is important is also essential.

9 It's not clear whether the debate over eating meat in Romans 14 is the "meat sacrificed to idols" debate of 1 Corinthians 8, a debate over whether the Mosaic dietary laws should still be followed (with meat avoidance being an easy way to do that), or some other controversy. Paul's use of the word "unclean" in 14:14 suggests that it had something to do with ceremonial law, which leads to the second of these options.

10 The "days" in question may have been Sabbath days, Jewish holidays prescribed in the Mosaic law, or special days in pagan calendars such as feast days. If the meat controversy was about following Mosaic dietary laws, it would seem most likely that the "days" in question were Sabbath days.

I should note that categorizing which disagreements are legitimately "disputable" in your church is beyond the purview of this book. That would be an entire book in itself. But beyond these questionable disagreements, you can probably tabulate a host of disagreements in your church that you *know* do not justify a church split nor necessitate leaving a church. You understand that theoretically you *should* be able to do church with those people, but it's hard. How can you love *them* with the genuine love of Romans 12?

Categorizing the Disagreement

Sometimes, simply understanding the dynamics of a particular disagreement can help root out judging and despising. See if you can recognize the disagreements that trouble you most in the following four categories, which I intend to be a reasonably comprehensive taxonomy of "disputable matters."

- *Sin for one person but not for another.* That is, consciences disagree on the morality of the thing itself. Or to quote Paul in Romans 14, "It is unclean for anyone who thinks it unclean" (14:14). For example, eating a specific food could be sin for one Christian (because his conscience forbids it) but not for another (whose conscience is free). Some church members believe it is sinful to work on Sunday. Some believe it's sinful to drink alcohol. In many cases, a Christian may *believe* that all who differ with him in this conviction are in sin, but a church need not divide over issues in this category.
- *The best way to achieve an agreed-on good.* That is, morality of the goal is not debated, but the path to get there is

unclear. A good example in this category is how society should combat racism or abortion, and what role the church should play in these efforts. Everyone in the conversation agrees that racism and abortion are evil. But they disagree on the best path toward justice. Disagreements over child-rearing also fall in this category. "I can't believe you let him play so many video games." Everyone agrees on the desired goal: raising our children in the discipline and instruction of the Lord (Eph. 6:4). But convictions differ on the best way to get there.

- *Different moral prioritizations.* In this case, what's unclear is how different moral goals trade off against each other. This third category is familiar in disagreements over how we spend our money. We all know it's important to give to our church and we all know it's important to provide well for our families. But one family's relative prioritization of those two values results in a car purchase that's "just too flashy, extravagant, and frankly, poor stewardship" in the eyes of another. Disagreements over voting often fall into this category, as we pick between candidates who offer us preselected baskets of moral goods.

- *Overlapping jurisdictions of authority.* That is, it's not clear who has moral authority. Let me explain with an example. Who's responsible to make sure a child is safe? Her parents, you say. But what if a parent is abusive and endangers that child's safety? Then, according to most Christians, the government has a role to play. God has given to parents the responsibility to raise their children *and* he has given to government the responsibility to protect its citizens. Whenever the jurisdiction of one God-given authority (the parents) overlaps with another (the government), Christians can arrive at very different positions of conscience because they *both* have Scripture on their side. Disagreements in this category are less common than in the first three, but they certainly are tricky!

Of course, as useful as it can be to understand the nature of our disagreements, we'll need more help than this if we're to love each another well. Very often what we need is a different vantage point from which to view the disagreement. In the previous chapter I discussed one such perspective in Romans 14—the faith of those you disagree with—now it's time to examine another.

Consider the Judge

In Romans 14:10, Paul asks the provocative question, "Why do you pass judgment on your brother? Or you, why do you despise your brother? For we will all stand before the judgment seat of God." This perspective of God's judgment is one we don't often consider, but we should. As we progress through the final chapters in Romans, and threats to unity become more morally fraught, Paul increasingly points us to God's final judgment. In fact, in this short chapter on convictional disagreement, Paul mentions our final accounting before God six different times (14:4, 10, 12, 18, 22, 23). These references fall into two categories. First, we should be conscious of God's imminent judgment of *others* because he's the judge and we're not (14:4). And second, we should be conscious of God's imminent judgment of our *own* lives (14:12). Both categories are crucial if judging and despising are to give way to genuine love.

God's Judgment of "Them"

First, let's look at God's judgment of others. Note that this is different from the "vengeance is mine" argument that we looked at in the chapter on forgiveness. Here, the "judgment" Paul has in view is not one of punishment but of accounting. As he asks in Romans 14:4, "Who are you to pass judgment on the servant of another? It is before his own master that he stands or falls. And he will be upheld, for the Lord is able to make him stand." It's not your responsibility to adjudicate all false opinions in your church. God will do that. Beyond that, even those in the wrong will still be standing at the end of judgment day because of their faith in Jesus Christ.

Now, remember that Paul is speaking of *debatable* matters. He's quite clear elsewhere in Scripture that more serious disagreements must be confronted (e.g., Gal. 1:9), and that the elders of a church are specifically tasked with this kind of correction (Titus 1:9). Also remember that in the right circumstances, love involves rebuke, even in areas that are legitimately disputable. As Proverbs states, "Better is open rebuke / than hidden love" (27:5). In fact, love often *compels* admonition (Matt. 18:15). For example, if the "weak" Christians of Romans 14 were not merely insisting that they themselves abstain from meat, but that Gentiles must do the same, Paul would not be advocating for unity but instead, as he does in Galatians, he would be rebuking them sharply for denying the gospel.

But those caveats notwithstanding, your role is to love, not to judge. *God* will settle this, so you don't need to. And—here's the kicker—no matter your poor opinion of this person's convictions, in God's final assessment the beauty of his or her faith will be magnificent.

When you're struggling to love those who approve what you understand is wrong, ask yourself whether this is a disagreement that should split your church. That is, is it a first- or second-level issue, to use Naselli and Crowley's categories? If not, then ask yourself a second question: Can you continue growing at your church despite the presence of this disagreement? That's a question that you would be wise to answer in consultation with Christians you trust. Hopefully reading this book has increased your ability to thrive amidst disagreement at church. Yet in humility and honesty, we must sometimes say, "If my faith were stronger, I could stay on in this church. But given my current level of maturity, I need to go elsewhere."

Very often, however, this disagreement need not split your church, and it need not split you off from your church. In those situations, God's judgment of those you disagree with is an empowering perspective. God's coming judgment reminds us that these debates need not be settled in this life. Yes, conversation and debate *can* be useful, letting "iron sharpen iron." Yet for such disagreements, do not exhaust yourself in argument. Instead, prioritize unity.

I'm reminded of a comment a friend made about a disagreement about which he felt quite passionate. "When we get to heaven, we'll see who was right—*if we even care then.*"[11] Such a humble perspective! The issues that threaten to divide us today,

---

11 Isaac Adams, "Remember, Christians Won't Always Fight & Quarrel," United? We Pray website, May 27, 2021, https://uwepray.com/.

that provoke judging and despising, may well feel relatively unimportant when they're settled in glory.

God's Judgment of You

Then there's a second corrective that God's future judgment provides. Not only must you consider *their* accounting before God, but you must consider your own. While we will not be condemned for our sin if we are in Christ (Praise God, Jesus paid its penalty [Rom. 8:1]!), a final evaluation of our lives still awaits: "Each of us will give an account of himself to God" (Rom. 14:12).

The reality of God's future judgment forces a brilliant reprioritization of what is "wrong" in your church. As Paul says in 14:20, "Everything is indeed clean, but it is *wrong* for anyone to make another stumble by what he eats." In this debate about food, Paul tells those with freer consciences that they're right, and those who can't eat meat are wrong. And yet . . . what's *really* wrong is an insistence on Christian freedom to eat meat in front of them. (Contemporary debates over alcohol come to mind.) Or consider verse 15: "By what you eat, do not destroy the one for whom Christ died." What strong language! Yes, these people will find out on judgment day that their consciences were too narrow. But you will face a much stricter accounting for your failure to bear with them in love. This brings to mind some of Martin Luther's opening lines in his treatise on Christian freedom: "A Christian is a perfectly free lord of all, subject to none. A Christian is a perfectly dutiful servant of all, subject to all."[12] Freedom in Christ, yes—and with it, the delightful bondage of love.

12 Martin Luther, *On Christian Liberty* (Minneapolis, MN: Fortress Press, 2003), 2.

Consider four ways in which your final accounting before God can change the posture of your heart toward those with whom you disagree, to whom you are bound in love.

1. Prioritization. Passages like Romans 14 push the priority of various disagreements a few steps into the background and the unity of the church into the foreground. As Paul says in Romans 14:22, "Blessed is the one who has no reason to pass judgment on himself for what he approves." When your heart is in the thick of judging and despising, look to your Judge. Remember that you will likely face a stricter judgment for failing to disagree in love than you would if you'd simply argued the wrong side of the disagreement.

2. Freedom. For some, it feels disingenuous to pursue a friendship at church while ignoring a festering disagreement. But Paul's prioritization of such disagreements relative to unity and love gives us freedom to do just that. It probably isn't wise to *never* discuss your disagreement. But with God's final judgment in view, you *can* pursue such friendships without resolving your disagreements.

3. Peace. By which I mean peace in your heart that expels anger. Very often it's God's judgment that we must remember when we're angry with others at church. Just as smoke indicates fire, anger indicates injustice. The question is how you'll respond to that injustice. Will you spin your heart into a whirlwind of self-righteous contempt by endlessly rehearsing to yourself arguments against those you disagree with? Or will you quench your anger in God's soothing promise to one day settle all wrongs?

4. Love. Remember the generative power of forgiven sin. When judging and despising emerges in your heart, don't just try to push it back down or ignore it. Confess it, using the strong language that Paul uses here. "Lord, I confess to you that in my attitude toward Omar, I'm seeking to destroy one for whom you died." "Lord, I confess that in my judging of Sherri, I'm creating stumbling blocks to her affection for you." Confess your sin, exult in your forgiveness, and delight as forgiveness turns your heart toward love. "Be wretched and mourn and weep. . . . Humble yourselves before the Lord, and he will exalt you" (James 4:9–10).

Escape from Judging and Despising into Love

Our hearts are a mess, aren't they? They are full of judging and despising. That's why we so desperately need to consider what Paul gives us in Romans 14. We must consider faith, especially the faith of those we disagree with. And we must consider God's judgment, both the final accounting of those we disagree with and our own. This is not a paint-by-number plan to guarantee immediate love. But as you immerse yourself in these truths, God's word will be at work to humble, reshape, and reform you.

It's fitting, then, that this section ends with a poignant re-minder of God's love for us: "Welcome one another as Christ has welcomed you, for the glory of God" (15:7). With this, Paul finishes this section where he began it in Romans 14:1, telling us to welcome those who are weak in faith. But now we see its result: "the glory of God." Is this not what we want in our churches? As we welcome those who disagree with us because Christ has wel-comed them, God's glory shines more brightly than if we never disagreed in the first place.

Questions for Reflection and Discussion

1. What do we know from Scripture about the final accounting before God that Christians will one day experience? (See John 5:24 and Rom. 8:1 and then Rom. 14:10; 2 Cor. 5:10; and Heb. 4:12–13.)

2. How can we tell the difference between disputes in the church that we should work to settle and disputes where we should "agree to disagree," leaving them to God?

3. Recall the four ways that our final accounting before God should change our posture toward others (prioritization, freedom, peace, love). Which resonates most with you? Why?

Prayer Points

- Pray that you would live in view of your final accounting before God (Rom. 14:10).
- Pray that people in your congregation would not cause each other to stumble by how they respond to differences in conviction (Rom. 14:20).
- Pray that the teachers of your church would be sobered by the stricter accounting that they will one day experience (Heb. 13:17; James 3:1) and that they would find confidence in Christ to serve in light of that accounting.

Christ" (Rom. 15:5–6). But there's a reason Paul prays to the "God of endurance and encouragement." We will need both if we're to live out this vision for our churches.

With that slightly overwhelmed feeling in mind, let's conclude with Paul's final prayer that closes out this lengthy section on love. After reminding us of God's promise from ancient times that Jew and Gentile would come together in Christ, Paul prays in Romans 15:13, "May the God of hope fill you with all joy and peace in believing, so that by the power of the Holy Spirit you may abound in hope." Do you hear his repeated reference to *hope*? Hope is in fact a primary theme in the closing verses of this treatise on love. Hope comes as we persevere in love (15:4). Hope comes as we see Christ's example of persistent love laid out in the Scriptures (15:4). And such hope is indispensable if we are to welcome one another as Christ has welcomed us (15:7)—even those with whom we disagree (15:1).

Hope, after all, is an essential ingredient to Christian fellowship. Whereas our world builds community that's rooted in the past, Christians must learn to root it in the future. Consider for a moment how often our world anchors community in the past. The color skin you were born with, your country of origin, the place where you studied, your professional background, seminal experiences in your life, past hurts, past triumphs—all these serve as foundations for community in this world's eyes. In fact, our modern culture is increasingly telling us that the past is an *inescapable* source of identity. Yet if the eyes of these Roman Christians had been trained on their past identity as Jew or Gentile, the harmony of Romans 12–15 would not have been possible. Nor would this harmony be possible for us. Thus Paul's interest in hope.

Hope in What?

What exactly is the future event that Paul prays we will look forward to with hope? The verse just prior to the prayer we've been discussing is the answer. In Romans 15:12, Paul quotes Isaiah's prophesy that as the Gentiles put their hope in Jesus, the coming reign of Christ will be one not of judgment but of salvation. As such, the hope Paul has in mind looks ahead to the day when God's people in their fullness—Jew *and* Gentile—will have all been brought in (Rom. 11:12, 25). This is so much more certain than the temporal hopes that often undergird our love at church: hope that "we'll get better at this" or "they'll mature" or "time will heal." Instead, Paul's prayer is that through hope that Jew and Gentile will *one day* praise God with united voice, they will realize *today* a peace and harmony that glorify God.[1]

Paul prays that this hope will lead to joy. If you want to move from avoiding "those" people, to loving them out of obligation, to loving them with joy, then you must learn how to root your friendships not in the past but in the future; that is, in the future you share with them in Christ Jesus. You cannot define those who "drive you crazy" based on the past, just as these Roman Christians could not define each other by their Jewish or Gentile heritage. Instead, you must define these people based on their future. Your love must be rooted in hope.

And what is the result? More hope! "So that by the power of the Holy Spirit you may abound in hope" (Rom. 15:13). In a virtuous cycle, hope begets hope. Hope in God's promised future

---

1   Douglas Moo, *The Epistle to the Romans*, The New International Commentary on the New Testament (Grand Rapids, MI: Eerdmans: 1996), 881.

empowers joy-filled peace among the diverse children of God through the power of the Spirit, and as this shadow of our future comes into focus, we abound in hope.

Promises to Give Us Hope

Let's consider then how each of the eight truths that we've culled so far from Paul's teaching in Romans can flavor our love at church with the hope of God.

- *Truth 1: Insistence on unity displays the glory of God.* At times all you can see of your church with the naked eye is disagreement, dissention, and turmoil. But through faith we have hope that God is painting a portrait of his glory far more stunning than if everyone were on the same page to begin with.
- *Truth 2: Impossible love flows from impossible mercy.* When God asks you to love beyond your own strength, he also gives hope that the power behind your love is not your own virtue but his own, inexhaustible mercies.
- *Truth 3: Disunity at church lies about Jesus.* Because God has staked the reputation of his dear Son on the unity of your church, you can take hope that what he is doing in your church really is "good and acceptable and perfect" (Rom. 12:2).
- *Truth 4: You belong together.* In God's providence, the words "members one of another" (Rom. 12:5) are an invitation, offering hope that, as you continue to seek Christ together as a church, you will discover how suited you really are for each other.

- *Truth 5: Hope in God creates affection for others.* Hope in God's purposes for "those people" is the road to joy in "those people"—the joy Jesus experiences in his love for you.
- *Truth 6: Divine justice empowers full forgiveness.* Just as God's mercy empowers love, God's justice empowers forgiveness. His perfect justice offers hope that your forgiveness of others can be the full and glorious "anti-fair" forgiveness of God.
- *Truth 7: People you dislike often act in faith.* Yes, your church may be brimming with disagreements over what is right and what is just. But their faith in Christ provides hope that even convictional disagreement is no barrier to genuine friendship and fellowship.
- *Truth 8: We will answer to God.* God's promise to judge gives hope that what is true will one day be beyond dispute. This means that in disagreements over "disputed matters" in the church (Rom. 14:1), we need not quarrel but can act in love.

Jesus is creating a stunning picture of his glory in your church, and no matter your flaws and failings, he will succeed! Jesus is creating a stunning picture of his glory through the faith of those you struggle to love, and he will succeed. Jesus is creating a stunning picture of his glory through *your* faith-filled love, as imperfect as it may be. And he will succeed. This is the hope we have through faith in Christ. This is the hope that makes the road I've described in this book a *joy* to travel. This hope is that God is at work in all things, and that in all things his work is good.

C. S. Lewis said it well: "The Church has no beauty but what the Bridegroom gives her; He does not find, but makes her, lovely."[2]

So put on your "faith glasses," my friend. Put on your faith glasses to marvel at the beautiful portrait of Christ that he is painting in your church. And where your vision fails you, trust that one day you will rejoice at all that God has done.

Questions for Reflection and Discussion

1. What does it look like to emphasize future commonality more than past commonality in relationships at church?

2. What is the hope Paul has in mind in Romans 15:12–13? How should that hope change your outlook on difficult relationships at church?

Prayer Points

- Pray that the hope you have in God's promises would forever change how you view the people in your church.
- Pray that your congregation would believe the hope-filled promises that God has given about their future as God's people.
- Pray that through hope-filled faith, there would be joyful peace between the leaders of your church.

---

2   C. S. Lewis, *The Four Loves* (1960; New York: Harcourt Brace & Company, 1988), 105.

Afterword

Under the Surface of a "Christ Alone" Church

A Few Words about Church Structure

THIS BOOK HAS BEEN about how relationships at church can show off the power of the gospel when we discover that sharing Christ is enough to be in fellowship despite differences of background, personality, opinion, and even conviction. As such, this book has focused on you at an individual level, since you're the one building all those Jesus-exalting, difference-defying relationships. I hope that you've found my reflections on Paul's wisdom in Romans to be a useful aid in this endeavor.

But the Scriptures don't intend for all this to happen merely at the level of individual relationships. The structure of the local church can help. When a church follows the commands and patterns laid out for it in Scripture, it is fertile soil for the kinds of relationships I've described in this book. Or, to switch analogies, a rightly ordered church is like having the wind at your back as you seek to build relationships where you share little in common other than Christ.

For the next few pages, then, let me take you on a brief tour of the inner workings of your church so you can see how these structures can foster the kind of church community Paul describes in Romans 12–15. Perhaps with all the instruction of the preceding chapters fresh in your mind, you'll have a new appreciation for these aspects of a church as you see the relational dividends they produce. And perhaps you'll be able to better use these structures as you seek to "with one voice glorify the God and Father of our Lord Jesus Christ" (Rom. 15:6). Let's examine five elements of a church to see how they accomplish this.

Expositional Preaching

Christians often distinguish between two types of preaching: "topical" preaching, where the message is about a particular topic (e.g., what the Bible says about friendship), and "expositional" preaching, where the message explains and applies a particular passage of Scripture. In expositional preaching the point of the message is the point of the passage. Both topical and expositional preaching can be useful for a church, but a church will do best if most of its preaching is expository in nature. Why is that? First, when the main diet of a church is topical preaching, the congregation rarely learns more than what the pastor already knows. But when that pastor is faithfully preaching through the whole of God's inspired word, he is also learning, with the agenda set by Scripture. Second, expositional preaching not only encourages and exhorts the congregation, but it unpacks for them a passage of Scripture that can continue encouraging and exhorting them long after the sermon is finished. Everything I've described in this book requires faith. Faith comes from God's word (Rom. 10:17). As such, a preaching ministry that's centered on God's word and not a pastor's ideas (no matter how wise) is an immense aid to faith-fueled relationships.[1]

Corporate Prayer

The preaching I just mentioned is one way in which God normally fuels relationships of supernatural breadth and depth in his church. Prayer is the other. Nothing I've described in this book can be done without the Spirit's aid. If it could, then how would it point to God and his glory? If we want to love the ones who drive us crazy, then we must be filled with the Spirit's love for them—and that is something only God can do. Thankfully, one great privilege of the Christian is God's promise to answer our prayers. As Jesus said, "Whatever you ask in my name, this I will do, that the Father may be glorified in the Son" (John 14:13). That's one reason why each chapter in this book has ended with three points of prayer: one for you as an individual, one for your congregation, and one for the leaders of your church. As William Gurnall noted, "The Christian's armour will rust, except it be furbished and scoured with the oil of prayer."[2]

Yet ideally, prayer for the life of your church shouldn't be confined to your individual times of prayer. God gets great glory

---

1   For further reading see David Helm, *Expositional Preaching: How We Speak God's Word Today* (Wheaton, IL: Crossway, 2014).
2   William Gurnall, *The Christian in Complete Armour* (1662; Carlisle, PA: Banner of Truth, 2002), 2:289.

when the entire church comes together to pray for his work of supernatural renewal to transform our relationships and love for each other. Prayer is an ordinary means to accomplish supernatural ends. You might take some of the prayer points I've listed in this book (or some of your own, drawn from Romans 12–15) and email them to your pastor as suggestions of what your church could pray for when it assembles together.[3]

A Biblical Understanding of Conversion

How does someone become a Christian? That may seem like an exceedingly basic question for a book like this, but too often churches assume the answer rather than teach it clearly. A good summary of what it means to become a Christian is found in Jesus's first words in the book of Mark: "Repent and believe the good news" (Mark 1:15). That is, have faith in his work for you (rather than relying in any way on your own good works), and see genuine faith result in a life of repentance from sin in order to follow Christ. This means that praying a prayer, walking an aisle, responding to an altar call, raising your hand with "every head bowed and every eye closed" does not make you a Christian. Those things may have been involved in your conversion, but they themselves are not conversion. To be converted, as Jesus said to Nicodemus, is to be born again (John 3:3). This is something that *God* must do; no sinner can simply wake up one morning and say, "Today I'm going to be born again."

When churches assure those who have walked an aisle/prayed a prayer/raised a hand that they are now born again simply because

---

3 For further reading see John Onwuchekwa, *Prayer: How Praying Together Shapes the Church* (Wheaton, IL: Crossway, 2018).

they did something, they often fill their pews with people who honestly *think* they are Christians but who have never been taught clearly what it means to become a Christian. And as I mentioned in the introduction, this book presumes that the "ones who drive you crazy" are in fact Christians. If they are not, much of this book will be exceedingly difficult to apply. A church's biblical teaching on how someone becomes a Christian is an important aspect of building Spirit-filled relationships that beautifully reflect the glory of Christ.[4]

Meaningful Membership

I mentioned back in the first chapter that the kind of relationships I've described in this book are entirely antithetical to a consumeristic "What's in this for me" mentality. Well, church membership is the formalization of this anti-consumer ethos. When you join a church, you make big promises (to love one another, encourage one another, submit to one another, etc.) to a group of people you probably don't yet know very well. You commit to love them, even the ones who drive you crazy. You submit to their authority as a congregation. You accept church on Jesus's terms and not on your own. Why would you do that? To quote 1 John 4:19: "We love because he first loved us."

On the other hand, if membership doesn't exist or is only loosely maintained and each person relates to the congregation in whatever way he or she thinks is best, everything I've described in this book is that much harder. The infrastructure of membership (statements of faith, membership interviews, member meetings,

---

4   For further reading see Michael Lawrence, *Conversion: How God Creates a People* (Wheaton, IL: Crossway, 2017).

etc.) will vary between churches. Yet the basic concept of membership is one that is important for all churches. It involves two things. First, meaningful membership requires that members give credible evidence of faith in Jesus Christ. That is, they seem to be Christians and, when they sin, they repent of it. Second, meaningful membership requires that members commit to one another as Scripture calls them to in all its "one another" commands. Though the analogy of a marriage covenant isn't exact for a number of reasons, it does parallel church membership in this regard. Just as the commitment of marriage formalizes and protects the relationship between husband and wife, the commitment of membership formalizes and protects the relationship between Christian and congregation.[5]

Biblical Church Discipline

This last element of church structure is one that Jesus clearly calls us to (see Matt. 18:15–20), and it's the logical companion to meaningful membership. If a church is to be a beautiful reflection of her Savior, then its membership must be comprised of those who give credible evidence of having been born again. But Jesus was clear that there are "many" who, while thinking they are his followers, are not in fact Christians (Matt. 7:15–23). Sometimes we bring into church membership those who at the time seem to be Christians, but over time their refusal to repent of serious sin suggests that they love their sin more than Jesus. That's when a church needs to follow Jesus's instructions in Matthew 18, 1 Corinthians 5, and elsewhere to lovingly confront

5   For further reading see Jonathan Leeman, *Church Membership: How the World Knows Who Represents Jesus* (Wheaton, IL: Crossway, 2012).

this person about his spiritually dangerous position. If he continues to refuse to repent, then eventually he should be put out of the church's membership. This doesn't mean that the person necessarily isn't a Christian (we hope he really is), but it is a vote of "no confidence" on the person's profession of faith since the fruit his life produces is not the fruit of faith. Note, of course that the title of this section is *Biblical* Church Discipline. Sadly, church discipline is often practiced in ways that do not follow biblical principles and as a result can be terribly destructive. On this topic, I recommend Jonathan Leeman's little book *Church Discipline* or, to understand how discipline fits into an ethos of biblical love, *The Rule of Love*.[6]

When churches fail to take on the hard work of church discipline, they will likely over time become increasingly comprised both of those who give evidence of faith and those who don't. And, as Paul warns us in 1 Corinthians 5:6, "A little leaven leavens the whole lump." Church discipline is not retributive; it is restorative in its purpose (1 Cor. 5:5). Hopefully it happens very occasionally. Yet it is an important part of protecting gospel witness in a congregation. Members of a church must *be* in Christ if they are to *find unity* in Christ.

The Importance of Structure

If you hear your pastor talking about some of these things, he hasn't simply gotten lost in theological minutiae. He's trying to tilt the basic structures of your church toward the thing that matters

---

6   Jonathan Leeman, *Church Discipline: How the Church Protects the Name of Jesus* (Wheaton, IL: Crossway, 2012); and *The Rule of Love: How the Local Church Should Reflect God's Love and Authority* (Wheaton, IL: Crossway, 2018).

General Index

Scripture Index

IX 9Marks

Building Healthy Churches

9Marks exists to equip church leaders with a biblical vision and practical resources for displaying God's glory to the nations through healthy churches.

To that end, we want to see churches characterized by these nine marks of health:

1. Expositional Preaching
2. Gospel Doctrine
3. A Biblical Understanding of Conversion and Evangelism
4. Biblical Church Membership
5. Biblical Church Discipline
6. A Biblical Concern for Discipleship and Growth
7. Biblical Church Leadership
8. A Biblical Understanding of the Practice of Prayer
9. A Biblical Understanding and Practice of Missions

Find all our Crossway titles and other resources at 9Marks.org.

vailable from 9Marks

For more information, visit **crossway.org**.